12⁵⁰

Tales My Father Never Told

The John Ben Snow Prize

This prize is given annually by the Press for an original manuscript of nonfiction dealing with some aspect of New York State.

The Press is especially pleased to be able to award the 1995 prize to this new work by one of New York State's finest writers, Walter D. Edmonds. *Tales My Father Never Told* has all the qualities this award has aspired to honor over the past seventeen years. The Press welcomes this new addition to our list of distinguished previous winners.

Past recipients include:

1978 *Warrior in Two Camps*
      William H. Armstrong

1979 *Black Education in New York State*
      Carleton Mabee

1981 *Joseph Brant, 1743–1807*
      Isabel Thompson Kelsay

1983 *Gustav Stickley, the Craftsman*
      Mary Ann Smith

1986 *Proud Patriot*
      Don R. Gerlach

1987 *Old-Time Music Makers of New York State*
      Simon J. Bronner

1989 *Landmarks of Oswego County*
      Judith Wellmann

1990 *Clear Pond*
      Roger Mitchell

1991 *Women's Humor in the Age of Gentility*
      Linda A. Morris

1992 *Make a Way Somehow*
      Kathryn Grover

1994 *Special Love/Special Sex*
      Robert S. Fogarty, editor

Tales My Father
Never Told

Walter D. Edmonds

SYRACUSE UNIVERSITY PRESS

Copyright © 1995 by Walter D. Edmonds

All Rights Reserved

First Edition 1995

95 96 97 98 99 00   6 5 4 3 2 1

Illustrations courtesy of the author.

"Fishing with a Fly" was previously published in the January 1983 issue of *Sports Illustrated* under the title, "A Birthday to Remember," and a small portion of "My First Drunk" appeared in the Fall 1982 issue of *Cricket.*

The paper used in this publication meets the minimum requirements of American National Standard for Information Sciences—Permanence of Paper for Printed Library Materials, ANSI Z39.48-1984. ∞™

Library of Congress Cataloging-in-Publication Data
Edmonds, Walter Dumaux, 1903–
    Tales my father never told / Walter D. Edmonds.
        p. cm.
    ISBN 0-8156-0307-X (cl.) — ISBN 0-8156-2657-6 (cl ltd ed : alk. paper)
        1. Edmonds, Walter Dumaux, 1903– —Family. 2. Novelists, American—20th century—Family relationships. 3. Fathers and sons—New York (State)—Biography. I. Title.
PS3509.D564Z464 1995
813\.52—dc20   94-34965

Manufactured in the United States of America

For Liz

who on a dark morning came through my door
and brought hope and love

Walter D. Edmonds is the award-winning author of more than thirty books. Some of the best known are *Drums Along the Mohawk, Chad Hanna,* and *Rome Haul.* His many novels and stories about upstate New York have made him one of this region's greatest writers. He lives in Concord, Massachusetts.

Contents

Preface

W hy should anyone set out to write a memoir such as this about the relationship between my father and myself from my early-digit years until his death near the end of my second year in college? Why write a memoir anyhow? I can't answer because I did not set out to write a memoir. My intention was to tell a few stories about times when he and I found ourselves at cross-purposes. I hoped they would be entertaining.

Memoirs should be the celebration of greatness, of great men and women whose lives have affected human history, of great love, of scientific discovery, of wisdom that enabled society to improve the quality of life. Let my readers, if any, be warned. There is nothing of that in these pages. My father and I were fifty-three years apart and understanding was not easy to come by. The episodes, per force, are told from my point of view. But if we did not often understand each other then, in the end I was able to see that love had existed, existed on both sides, and perhaps that disclosure is justification for this small book.

The writing did not come easily. Perhaps it would be more accurate to say that with a few exceptions these episodes were not easy to remember. I wrote the first two in 1981 and 1982: "My First Drunk" and "Fishing with a Fly." "Beginning" came along near the end, when I knew I was writing a memoir of my father and myself and was trying to find something about him in which I had no part, nor did I have to worry about being fair. The other chapters, as I have said, are all written from my point of view—hopefully maturing bit by bit as the years mounted.

There was a fifty-three year gap between his age and mine. I simply was not equipped to understand him, though towards the end I may have had a dawning awareness of the ramifications, mental and physical, of old age that made my behavior incomprehensible to him, as, for that matter, his often was to me. Yet even now seventy years later, when I myself have had to live with those very ramifications, he remains in many ways an enigma.

Sorting through box after box of family letters during evenings of two autumns when I was alone at Northlands, I came across the report of a handwriting expert to whom Mother had sent a sample of my father's writing. His report was in many ways remarkable; it covered so many facets of Father's character: his self-esteem, his love of clothes, his self-confidence in conjunction with insecurity. It described a man capable of great cruelty, but also of acts of quixotic generosity. And that undeniably was so, as I had learned over the years. His temper, the report suggested, had a very low flashpoint. That brought back to my memory a summer evening long ago when I was, I suppose, about ten years old.

I was sitting at the far end of the front verandah—Father insisted on our use of "verandah"; the kitchen door might open on a porch, but not the front. I was fresh from the bathtub and in clean clothes—another insistence of Father's, especially in my case because of my interest in the farm animals as well as all things pertaining to the barns. I was relaxing in the consciousness of rectitude, when a rig behind a single horse came up the drive. A youngish man, whom I spotted at once as a traveling salesman, hopped out and tramped up the steps to the front door on which he knocked thunderously and demanded of our waitress to speak to the lady of the house. When Mother came to the door, he announced that he was an agent of the Singer Company.

"Sewing machines," he said. Mother said she owned a Singer with which she was quite satisfied.

"How do you know you are?" demanded our caller, reaching for the wire handle of the screen door. But my mother, who seldom gave dust time enough to settle on her, had slipped the bolt under his nose. He became instantly angry and began to rattle and pound on the door.

At that moment the living room door, along the verandah near where I was sitting, slapped open and my father burst through in his shirt sleeves (he had been working on a brief) and roared in what I always imagined was his courtroom voice, "DON'T SPEAK TO MY WIFE LIKE THAT! Don't speak to ANY woman like that! DON'T SPEAK! Get off my property! GET OUT OF HERE!"

———————

"Who's going to make me, old man?" demanded the salesman.

"I am," my father said in a voice suddenly turned low and chilling. "Watty," he said (I had no idea he knew I was around), "Get me some stones down there along the ferns."

I jumped off the porch and began rooting them out of the ground with my newly-washed-for-supper fingers. "How big?" I asked.

"Egg size," said Father. "Quick, damn it. Or he'll get away." The salesman was backing down the steps. He no longer looked combative, but Father raised his voice to stentorian levels, calling on my brother, John, to fetch a rifle. "Load it," he shouted. "The .44-40."

I handed him another stone.

"Damn it," he said again. "I didn't say ostrich eggs! Hen's eggs, Watty!"

I handed him another stone. Father was no good at throwing, couldn't even skip a flat stone on water. The salesman, now getting into his wagon, was well out of Father's range. In a gesture of defiance and contempt he wheeled his horse across the lawn, leaving deep tracks, as he made his turn and started down the drive, suddenly whipping up his horse as John emerged from the house with the Winchester .44.

"It's loaded," John said. "Three cartridges."

Father grabbed it and ran out onto the driveway. For a moment I thought he was going to shoot the salesman. He was an absolute dead shot. But he pointed the muzzle to the sky and fired the three shots where there was not yet even a star. The old .44, with its large bore, made a prodigious noise and the salesman, now almost to the break of trees, took to his whip again. Father laughed. So, in my relief, did I. Mother came out on the verandah, too.

"You should not get so worked up, Gridgey," she said. "He meant no real harm."

"He spoke to you," Father said, "and I didn't like the way he did it."

I looked at him with fresh admiration and respect, and at the same time repressed a giggle.

His loyalty to his family was, like his shooting, absolute. So was the authority with which he governed our lives. Mother undoubtedly had ways of bringing him around, but a small son had no resources like hers. My brother declared his independence as soon as he got to college. On the farm the order of things changed markedly every fall when Father took the family back to New York City. The farmer's word, not Father's, became the law; I had no inclination then to step out on my own. He fascinated me. Like a bird in the eye of a snake, I was unable to tear myself free. Not that there was anything reptilian about my father. He was, I think, incapable of concealing his feeling. On a trip to Canada, on which he had taken Mother before their engagement (well chaperoned by a New York City judge and his wife) far up the Murray River, he disappeared from camp one Sunday afternoon. When Mother went looking for him, the guides, for whose benefit it was a day of rest, indicated that he had gone upstream. If she kept the river in sight or hearing, they said, she could not get lost. Mother went to seek him. He was sitting on a log when she found him, tears streaming down his cheeks, because, he finally told her, a man as old as he had no right to propose marriage to a woman as young and beautiful as she. What means she took or what she said is neither here nor there, but it must have been effective, for their engagement was announced within a week of their return to Philadelphia and New York. He was both a simple and a highly complicated man. He could be tender and he could be terrifying.

I tried in an earlier book, barely fictionalized, to write about him as he appeared to me when I was twelve. We were alone together one fall at the farm. The book is called *The South African Quirt*. It is in some ways a cruel and horrifying story. I wrote it entirely from my small boy's point of view. What is implicit—that in the novel the truly tragic figure is the father—was discerned by only two reviewers. What I have realized since is that I simply wasn't a good enough writer to get that point across while still maintaining the integrity of my small boy's point of view.

I sometimes wonder who could have done so. Shakespeare? Of course, if he had brought himself to deal with anything so small. Thackeray? Turgenev? Flaubert? And who in this country except Faulkner? Welty? As my father would have said, "Idle speculation." In his eyes the worst of my shortcomings was idleness and, as in many other things, he may have been right, for, when I observed to my mother during her final year that one of the difficulties of dealing with my young son was his laziness, my most gentle and ladylike parent, cheeks pink with indignation, reared herself up in bed and exclaimed, "Watty, you were the damnedest lazy little reptile I ever came across in all my life."

It has become apparent to me that I have written these two books for myself: the first to deal with, perhaps to extirpate, a cruel memory; the second to attempt to reach an understanding. And if it was not actually my design, that is what has happened. I have come to realize that in many ways he and I were very much alike. In *The South African*

Quirt my behavior was really very strange—as if I were baiting a caged bear, when the door of the cage was in fact unlatched and I knew it was unlatched. Yet I pursued my course with a determination almost suicidal. As for my father—well, for years I felt that many, perhaps most, people at one time or another in their lives walk on the edge of madness, and for Father that fall at Northlands was his walk.

In these *Tales* that madness fortunately does not repeat. Nor does my father ever fall prey to those chilling passions. And I am now able to see that throughout these episodes I was every bit as impliable as he; in truth, more so. Which makes me wonder how deep his repeated disappointment in me must have been. But I am also convinced that the love he felt was deep and real and that it worked both ways.

Concord, Massachusetts   Walter D. Edmonds
June 6, 1994

Tales My Father Never Told

East face of what the farm people called the big house. After I took on responsibility for the place the gray paint was changed to white for the three houses and red for the barns and outhouses—red with very dark green trim and white window sashes.

Beginning

A s I stood beside my father's bed looking down on his dead face on that first morning in May, 1924, I was overwhelmed by an impression that all his life he had been running scared. Death had softened the sternness. The opaque blue eyes that in an instant might turn icy were hooded by the closed lids. The lips, so often uncompromisingly set, looked vulnerable, like a small boy's. His face, so high in color as to seem on fire, was marble white, whiter now than the mustache and goatee whose whiteness in the living man were almost his personal trademark, like the trademarks he had spent his career defending to insure their integrity worldwide. A premonition of our being on the point of communication was abruptly obliterated by my awareness of the stillness. Then, faintly, through the open window, I heard the single muffled thud of a base drum.

At the foot of Fifth Avenue, at Washington Square, the first band to lead the May Day parade was on the point of stepping out. I was about to close the window when I recalled how Father loved to watch the marching men: regiment after regiment, each with a band, especially the Seventh, which was always led by Sousa's, their gray uniforms impeccable, their files from curb to curb perfectly aligned, every man six feet tall or better. No regiment marched like the Seventh. "Naturally," my father used to say. "After all, they are gentlemen." I could hear the brasses blaring as I closed the bedroom door and went to find my mother.

She was in her bedroom, sitting in a sunny window, sorting a basket of clean clothes that the laundress had just left with her. When I came in she was holding a pair of Father's woolen underdrawers against her cheek, her eyes full of tears. "It's hard to realize he is dead," she said. "He was so pleased to have beaten the pneumonia. When I came back after seeing Dr. Munroe out—about eight o'clock—I told him the doctor said he was out of danger. He smiled and asked me to roll a cigarette. I did, and lighted it, and put it in his mouth. In all our life together I never refused him," she said, as she had once before, her voice still very soft, almost forgiving, it seemed to me. "I left him puffing on it for ten minutes maybe. When I came back the cigarette had rolled out of his mouth, and he was dead. He had beaten the pneumonia. It was his heart that failed."

I was only partly right in my feeling that he had been running scared all through his life. It was not life, or the world he was scared of. It was himself and the fear that he might not measure up to his conception of masculinity, of being a man.

More than sixty years went by before I began to understand why. It was late one fall in the early 1980s. My wife had gone to England and our white Labrador and I were keeping house alone at Northlands. I decided to fill the evenings by going through old family correspondence stored in the attic for years in the sort of metal boxes that long ago had been used in legal offices for filing documents. There must have been two dozen; I opened them before the stove in my study. The stove front came off, bringing the fire into the room, as it were, and also affording easy disposal of such letters that it seemed to me better not to keep. Most of the letters were from my father to my mother at the farm and hers to him. But one evening I opened one box considerably larger than the rest, in fact a bread box that obviously had never seen the inside of a law office; and it turned out to contain material from the 1860s, about life in Utica, New York, as my father had experienced it in early boyhood.

The first item my fingers encountered was a very small—about two and a half inches by four—book, a diary of my father's for 1863, when he was twelve. It opened of itself to April 6, Wednesday: all of the tiny space allotted for that date was filled by a pencil sketch of a small dog of whom it might be said he was a sort of Sealyham—he, because just below was the name. Turbo.

My father was born in Utica to John Henry and Eugénie Doumaux Edmonds on the eighteenth of January, 1851. John Henry Edmonds was a prominent member of the bar of Central New York and a standing Master in Chancery, a title that before long became extinct with the abolition of the New York Court of Chancery. He was known also for a singular sweetness of temper which caused fellow citizens to address him affectionately as "Judge." Basically conservative, he had, however, impulses towards speculative enterprise, which his wife was to find alarming and, as we shall see, set out to combat.

Eugénie had been born in France in 1820 in Mauzen, a village in the valley of the Dordogne, the last of ten children. Her father, Jean Doumaux, was a wheat merchant, whose company failed when his partner absconded with all the funds of their business while Jean and his wife were making a first and only visit to Paris. To escape imprisonment for debt he fled to America with the six older children. Two years later Eugénie, with a brother, Hugh, and an old family servant, also left for America. Of all the big family only one sister, Mitte, remained in France; the mother had died in 1834, the year of Jean Doumaux's departure. Neither Hugh nor Eugénie ever saw their old home again.

They boarded ship at Le Havre. The voyage took seventy-three days, for their ship was dismasted during a storm and they spent twenty-three days lying off Fayal in the Azores while a new main mast was stepped. But eventually they reached New York City and set off to join their father at Martinsburg, a village in the Black River Valley of upstate New York. However, the family did not remain reunited for long. It was decided that Eugénie should continue her education and above all learn English. In the fall her brother Hugh took her to Schenectady where she entered Miss Sheldon's School for young Ladies, at which she spent a long, unhappy winter.

Many years later, near the end of her life, at the request of her granddaughters, she wrote a brief memoir which she titled *Autobiography of Eugénie Doumaux Edmonds* and in it she detailed the effect her introduction to the school had on her young French soul:

Never shall I forget my first meal at the school. Arriving after the usual dining hour, we were shown into the basement, for the dining-room was there, and there we saw a long table covered with oilcloth, two pronged forks, pewter tumblers, and piles of potato skins at each plate. My french ideas received such a shock, that I could not eat a bite. From that hour, I was homesick, until we moved in the spring to Utica, to establish The Utica Female Seminary. We all came up on a packet canal boat, Grandpa and Grandma Sheldon, teachers, scholars, servants, horse, cow, cats & dogs. As soon as I touched Utica soil my homesickness left me.

Which was just as well, for she was to live there for the rest of her life.

In the meantime the Doumaux family was once more fragmented. Hugh's health failed and he went to Texas, hoping to save it. Instead, he died there. Jean, the father, having failed at sheep farming on a dismal set of wilderness acres on the southern slopes of Tug Hill, returned to France where he remained in hiding until some years after Eugénie's marriage when once more he came to America to make his final home with her.

Hugh's death and her father's return to France left Eugénie sole alone and it was at this point that Miss Sheldon stepped in. She offered to let Eugénie finish her education free of charge if she agreed to continue with the school as a teacher of French until she had repaid her debt. It worked out well, as Eugénie noted in her memoir: "A native woman teacher was an exceptional thing in those days. My classes were large, my work most confining. Exercises to correct for 70 or 80 scholars was no small task."

Most of the work had to be done at night, "by the light of the miserable oil lamps we had in those days." And this was compounded by the world of English literature, opened to her by her newly gained knowledge of English. Her sight began to fail. She narrowly escaped blindness. "For six years I never read a book." She was shut up in a dark room, dosed with drugs, allowed only gruel and brown bread, until she became like the ghost of the vigorous French girl who had entered the school. Again Miss Sheldon took charge and sent her to stay with friends in New York City where, under proper medical care, her eyesight was restored.

Meanwhile she had repaid her debt to Miss Sheldon, "in less than two years, although the salary was very small." But, she added in her memoir, "I cannot pass on to other scenes, before saying what happy years those were, spent in that school, a perfect home. Miss Sheldon and her family were always lovely to me. I was one of them. Worlds fail me to express their kindness, or my gratitude."

The "other scenes" developed rapidly. The first was her change in religious allegiance. Born and raised a Catholic, she was on her way to Mass one Sunday morning when one of the sudden snowstorms that from time to time sweep down the Mohawk Valley struck Utica with blizzard force. Realizing that she could make way no farther along Genesee Street, she looked around for refuge and found herself within a few steps of Grace Episcopal Church. Gratefully she entered. A service was in progress, the congregation in prayer. Finding a place in a rear pew, she also knelt. Ahead of her she could identify many people she particularly admired and liked. Crossing herself as she finished her prayer, she rose from her knees an Episcopalian and remained a communicant of "Old Grace" to the end of her days.

In 1849 she met her future husband, became engaged, and married him four months later. As seems to have been the custom, the maid of honor and the best man accompanied the bride and groom on their wedding trip to Philadelphia and other points. Two children, my father and a sister, Annette, two years younger, were born in the first three years. The new parents at first rented a house on Bleecker Street, but in 1859 they moved into the house Eugénie was to spend the rest of her life in, on the east side of Chancellor Square, my father's boyhood home.

It was a house full of sunlight standing on a generous lot with room for a big garden, to the delight of old Jean Doumaux, who made it his special province. There was also a sizeable stable along whose south wall Eugénie, a person of determination, as we have already seen, espaliered fruit trees, producing pears, peaches, and even nectarines, which nobody in Utica, it seems, had done before. This accomplishment may or may not have inspired my father to dig his own small garden, though, like most children's, it ran largely to radishes and beets.

Life seems to have been tranquil enough there, though minor tensions might crop up, such as an April entry in my father's diary for 1863: "Beautiful morning today. Bob [perhaps a neighbor] and I have become enemies." Some happenings were matters of course: "May 1st: The Erie Canal is opened today." Or there might be an item of commercial interest: "Cloudy and cold and windy. At F. N.'s and E. P.'s request I bye one cent worth of molasses candy." Very occasionally there might be a notation of something grim. After mentioning a visit to Sulphur Springs, he wrote: "Margaret did drown the cat today in the canal." And two days later something grimmer yet: "The cat came home today from the canal." Like any small boy he pursued hobbies. On March 17: "I have been collecting stamps since November & have now 147 different kinds in a frame. I want to get J. Brondegee's Halvatia like everything."

Life in the house on Chancellor Square proceeded much like that in any normal house. The children had their meals separately, though now and then their old grandfather liked to join them, feeling with them no obligation to exercise his scanty English, and all three could chatter happily in French. When on feast days like Christmas, Easter, or Thanksgiving Day, they were allowed to join the adults in the dining room, the two children were not permitted to be seated but had to stand side by side at the foot of the table as they ate. Whether this was a custom Eugénie had brought with her from France, I do not know. I do know that my father remembered and resented it till the last years of his life.

A point still sorer in his memory was his first year of school. Because she considered his health fragile and because she was determined that he should have the best education available in Utica, she made up her mind to send him to her own old school—Miss Sheldon's Female Seminary. Some inkling of what it might be like to be the only boy in a flourishing establishment for young ladies must have come to her, but her own simple, as she thought, solution merely compounded her unfortunate decision. She dressed him as a girl to make him less conspicuous.

10

As it turned out young Walter, much as he loathed his situation, did not find being *in* the school unbearable; it was the daily journey to and from that broke him down. Neighborhood boys discovered in no time what was going on. They formed posses to pursue and taunt. In winter he was snowballed unmercifully. One snowball with an icy core broke his nose. Until he had passed well beyond Chancellor Square, he felt as terrified and lost as any captive pioneer running the gauntlet into an Iroquois town. It took nearly the school year for Eugénie to accept the fact that, instead of protecting the health of her son, her policy was actually destroying it. Reluctantly she withdrew him from Miss Sheldon's. In the following year he attended a school for boys.

One wonders, where was his father? What was he thinking? Why didn't he intervene? It seems to me that, like many men who marry women considerably younger than themselves, he had fallen utterly under the spell his wife cast over him. This applied in no small degree to his thinking as well as his emotions. An instance was her persuading him to alter the investment of his savings, which at the time of their marriage amounted to something between twenty and thirty thousand dollars, a not inconsiderable sum for those days in upstate New York. John Henry had invested nearly all of it in stock of the newly formed Utica and Schenectady Telegraph Company, which ultimately, I have been told, became one of the five parent companies of Western Union. Eugénie, who had seen her father go bankrupt, was convinced that the only safe place for savings was in land. So John Henry's nest egg, which might in time have hatched quite a fortune, was devoted instead to Oneida County second farm mortgages. One of the many that proved worthless was the Black River property that ended in my father's hands and became Northlands, where I was born.

———————

Except for his winter at a school for girls, young Walter, or Wat as the family called him, seems to have led a reasonably happy life. He was full of enterprise. In addition to his garden he was soon in the business of selling eggs—"strictly fresh"—to immediate neighbors. Apparently he did some investigating and came up with the notion that Spanish Blacks were superior to every other breed of hen. On August 24, 1863, he bought "five full-blooded black Spanish hens." With the assistance of "Mr. Richards and Ed," as he recorded, a yard had been constructed for their reception, as well as a small house with roosts and nests, in which he evidently took great pride. The venture succeeded well, as in a moment we shall see.

In spite of the small orbit in which he moved he did have initimations of other things beyond the confines of Utica. Early one spring morning in 1861 the rattle of snare drums woke him. From the window he saw in Chancellor Square a regiment of Zouaves, their huge scarlet pantaloons, made even redder than their natural color by the light of sunrise, were performing their celebrated dress parade. They had detrained at the depot to break their long journey from Chicago in answer to President Lincoln's call for volunteers. Father never forgot the precision of their drill nor their aura of invincibility.

And then, two years later, while the Civil War still raged, he went to City Hall to see Tom Thumb. "He is very small indeed," wrote the young diarist. "His wife is smaller than he is 32 inches high."

In August of the same year he had his first experience with firearms. "Spent the day at Uncle Francis and fire a gun for the first time in my life. I fire at a mark 3 time and hit it every time at the distance of two rods." It must have dawned on him then that even though he might be smaller than others, here was something at which he could excel. He begged his parents to let him have a gun. Eugénie refused point blank. This time his father backed him, yielding to Eugénie only in her demand that the gun be long enough in the barrel so that Wat could not pull the trigger if any other part of his anatomy was in front of the gun's mouth.

John Henry found an old muzzle-loader that met these specifications. It was so heavy that Walter could barely carry it. It was probably a good deal more dangerous than one of the appropriate length and weight would have been, for he had to drag it between the rails of the snake fences he climbed, pulling the barrel towards him with hammer and trigger scraping against the rails they passed between. Mercifully, no accident occurred. Regrettably, however, during those long summer days on Uncle Francis' farm, his principal quarry became the meadowlark of which with his unerring eye and steadily increasing skill he bagged many. They made delicious eating, which so pleased Eugénie that she became reconciled to having a sportsman for a son.

He remained a sportsman all his life, and whether hunting or fishing, it was vital that he should surpass all others. His eight-and-a-quarter-pound brook trout was, for many years, the largest caught in the Murray River in Quebec. And when my mother introduced him to his first born child, my brother John, proclaiming with tremulous pride that he weighed eight pounds and three ounces, Father reminded her that his trout was bigger. In the same vein he liked to remind us all his life that he had killed a bull caribou across a lake three-quarters of a mile long with a single shot. The animal's splendid head was mounted on the library wall, as was his great trout.

So we come back to the faded pencil drawing of the little dog named Turbo. He seems to have accounted for the only real tragedy in Walter's early life. The diary contains three entries, the first on April 6. "My little dog Turbo died today he had fits & he died in 1 hour. He was the best little fellow in the world. Poor Turbo we shall hear your little bark no more." On April 17, written in pencil instead of the usual ink, "Note 4 years after Poor Turbo I don't forget you by any means. The whining Spot that I have now is different indeed from you: of all dogs the best." And then, in an open space considerably earlier than April 6, what seems an almost capricious effort to try for a more affecting note, "My little dog Turbo died today of a sort of Pralyses he was the best little fellow that ever lived we buried him in my garden where he loved well to be," almost as if Wat was searching for a perfect epitaph. Even in his seventies Father spoke of Turbo now and then. I have no doubt that everything he said about the little dog was true. It was a real love, deeply felt. I think in his own mind the process of my father's growing up began with Turbo's death. An entry in the diary three years later could indicate as much:

> At this point this interesting narrative appears to end. The flock of 7 fowls spoken of has done well. I think that I have raised and bought about one hundred fowls since than and have now on my hands a flock of 40 with a market in view to Mr. Hefferon to whom I sold them last year at a dollar apiece.
>
> What a mistake I made when I called my hens full blooded I paid six shillings a pair for them for the ones I have now I paid 6 dollars.
>
> I gave up collecting postage stams 2 years ago after having got one of the best collections in town.
>
> I now go to Advanced school and hope to get transferred to the Academy (just building) 1 year about from now.
>
> It makes me laugh now to think of the great Sanjags minstrels & c What fun we had in those days.
>
> Since the time I fired the first gun at Uncle Francis I have become a great hunter My passion for the sport is immense Many is the partridge & black squirrel I have caused to bite the dust
>
> W D E

Quite obviously the sometimes awesome father I was to know when my time came was on his way to meet me.

Me at age seven, watching a "spinner" after it had left my hands.

My First Drunk

There is nothing, absolutely nothing, more revolting and squalid than a drunk—male or female, "my father proclaimed in the carrying voice he employed in court, causing my mother at the other end of the table, gently to remonstrate, "Now, Gridgey, do you think this is an appropriate subject for luncheon?" She used her pet name for him, a softening of "Grizzley" for grizzley bear.

"I do," Father replied. "Nobody is too young for that lesson to be driven home." He banged his hand down on the folded copy of our local weekly paper. "Here is a case in point." He put on his glasses and read, " 'On Wednesday last George Filmore came to this village and as usual imbibed of the spiritous, got drunk, and left for home on foot. Got tired, laid down on the road, and was run over by Charles Doty's lumber wagon with a ton of feed for his stock on it, breaking both Filmore's legs near the thighs. If this does not cure George of his propensity for strong drink, nothing will.' That is highly unlikely," my father continued. "George Filmore is a drunk, always was one, and will be until his death, which will probably occur much sooner than he imagines."

He turned his piercing blue eyes on me, as he usually did when making an observation on morals or behavior in general, the upturned points of his Kaiser-like mustache appearing to quiver. He had been fifty years old when he married for the first time, and I think now that he found his children—my older brother, myself at ten, and my five year old sister—to be at times almost incomprehensible beings. He must have been aware that he was unlikely to see any of us reach adulthood and it worried him to think what we might turn into. Especially me, whom he regarded as untruthful, irresponsible, and weak. Not that I was aware of this, only that I existed on the lower floors of his esteem.

"He will lose his legs," Father went on, "and be even more useless than he has been up to now. If you meet him, stay away from him. Stay away from any drunk. They are the lowest of the low."

He dipped his fingers in the finger bowl he insisted on having at every meal and passed them over his lips beneath the white mustache. My mother sighed and rose from her chair.

I went upstairs to my room and thought about what my father had said about the dreadfulness of drunkenness and about Mr. Filmore's having to have his legs sawed off, as I presumed would be the procedure. Staying away from him, it seemed to me, should not be difficult. I wondered what he would look like. I had a vague recollection of a man I had seen sitting on the grass in Washington Square a few winters ago (we spent the winters on 11th Street in New York City, and I had gone to the Square with the little girl next door and her nurse to play hopscotch). The man had looked helpless, staring blindly about him, and I recall two streams of liquid of some sort issuing from his nose, a fascinating if horrifying sight. But the nurse had quickly seized each of us by the hand and hustled us away, so I had only the briefest of impressions and had no idea of whether the man was indeed drunk or only sick. Thinking of him now, I felt vaguely glad that I did not know. I had no inkling that I would meet someone genuinely drunk within twenty-four hours.

The daily chore of taking the mail down to our rural box on the river road had been assigned to me that summer. At the start it had been an adventure. I put the letters in a canvas bag with a shoulder strap and set out with a feeling of importance. But as the summer went on and on into fall, my interest began to pall. I no longer carried the news from Ghent to Aix or galloped west for the Pony Express. I was bored and blasé that October morning. The unaccustomed white of our first killing frost crackling under foot meant nothing as I followed the narrow dirt track that served as our driveway across the home meadow and into the fifty yards of woodland the edged the river. I did notice that a lot of wild black cherries had fallen, presumably due to the frost. The road was carpeted with them and they squirted purplish juice on my sneakers, no matter how I tried to avoid them. Looking ahead I saw that they reached all the way to the river road and, picking his way among them, was a chipmunk.

At least that, at first glance, was what I thought he was doing. But it soon became clear that the oscillations of his wavering course were beyond his control. He was heading home, I felt sure, but it was anyone's guess if he would get there.

I knew where his hole was, almost opposite to where I was standing, in a low bank on the right of the road and framed by the roots of a yellow birch. During the summer I had seen him dozens of times, peering out as I went past or zipping back in like a well-directed arrow.

I dropped to my knees as he came closer, putting my head down until I as almost on his level, and saw that his cheek pouches were full to bursting, so swollen that he was barely able to keep them clear of the ground. A purple juice was oozing out the corners of his mouth and had stained all the front of him. He stopped as he came close to me and I saw his eyes focussing painfully on mine. He was about the most serious-looking chipmunk I had ever seen, or have seen in my sixty-odd years since. He showed no fear. Even at my early age I had a glimmering of what he saw me as: a great, looming shadow, a mysterious hulk, but nothing that, under his immediate problems, need concern him. I don't know whether chipmunks sneeze and he did not exactly do so, but he made a sort of squeak and a tiny purple spray blew out of his mouth and it seemed to me his eyes began to water. Then he turned to his left and wobbled across the driveway. At the far side he seemed to gain confidence. He had spotted the entrance to his home. He paused. I could see him laboriously draw in his breath, as heavy as a hand-pulled anchor. Then he made a rush for his hole.

He missed it. His nose struck into the sandy earth about an inch to right of it. He gave a hiccough and an extra squirt of cherry juice came out of him. He backed off and had another prolonged really careful look. He made a second rush, and missed again, this time hitting two inches to the left. It made him lose his balance and he rolled back to the edge of the road. But he remained undaunted. I could see him hauling in his breath again, and then another, and a third. He started forward. He could no longer raise his tail, so he let it drag. Somehow, and I think he was as astonished as I, he hit the hole dead center.

I was not to see him again for several days. Perhaps he was suffering a hangover, though I did not then know what that was. In fact I did not know that he was drunk until, after I'd told my story at lunch—acting out the chipmunk's bewildered motions with high gusto—that my father explained that the little beast must have been drunk. The cherries he had been carrying home had been fermented by the frost.

"You mean like Cherry Bounce?" I asked, thinking of the six-quart jars filled with painfully gathered wild black cherries and then covered to the brim with Scotch whiskey, which my father insisted on Mother's manufacturing each fall.

"Yes," said my father, "in a way."

"It sure made him bounce," I said, a little wildly. "Like Mr. Doremus last winter when he had four glasses." Mr. Doremus was an impecunious inventor for whom Father procured patents from time to time who had come to our house at 18 West Eleventh Street with another one of his

21

inventions. "Mr. Doremus just like the chipmunk," I cried. "Bounce, bounce, bounce. And then he went THUD!" For Mr. Doremus had suddenly found himself sitting on the floor.

"Leave the table!" my father ordered, using his court room voice. "I will not have any guest of mine so spoken of. LEAVE THE TABLE!"

As I got up to go my mother protested mildly.

"He didn't mean to insult Mr. Doremus, Gridgey. He only meant to be funny."

But Father was unrelenting. "It's time he learned that being fresh is not being funny."

And as I left the room I heard my brother intone:

"Watty is the family clown.
When he gets up, we knock him down."

Me with Prince Paladin Wayne, who turned out badly. Even then the men avoided him.

The Summer of the Sour Cream

It was in 1910 that we at Northlands, as Father had named our upstate farm, learned that we had to cooperate with The Other People. Maggie Corcoran was the person who told us how it was. There were, she said, the people who lived in our big rambling house; there were the people who lived in the two farm houses across the brook; and then there were The Other People. They lived in the brook and according to their way of thinking the brook belonged to them.

Whether fairies exist or do not exist has troubled the mind of the human race, if not its conscience, from the beginning of time. My father not unnaturally pooh-poohed the notion. He had bought the title to what became Northlands from his dead father's estate to bolster his widowed mother's cash account. The place and everything on it belonged to him. The idea that fairies, little creatures that really did not exist, could claim his brook as their own was an impossibility—sheer anathema to him. It was preposterous. It was anarchical. He would not permit it. But Maggie not only held to her convictions, she went on talking about The Other People as if they were a natural fact of life.

"But how can you be so sure?" asked Mother, whose one overriding ambition was to keep her household peaceful and contented.

"Oh, I see them," Maggie replied. "I see them going up and down upon their affairs." She hesitated, looking straight at Mother with a smile on her face. "And sure, Mem, doesn't the little man come into my room at night?"

"The little man?" Mother asked. "Who is the little man, Maggie?"

"Why, he's the mayor of them all, to be sure," Maggie answered. She had once, in childhood, seen the Mayor of Dublin whom she considered the greatest man on earth, "except for the Holy Father himself, of course," she hastened to add with an odd little motion halfway between a bow of her head and a curtsy.

"It seems strange they should call him their mayor when they have only a brook to live in," Mother observed.

"Oh, I guess it's because he tells them what they ought to do," Maggie said with another of her smiles. "Now, would you be planning the meals, Mem?"

Maggie Corcoran was our cook that summer. It was her second place since coming over from Ireland, and she was used to being in the country. "I can help with making the hay if you like," she told Mr. Hoyt, the farmer or "superintendent" as my father called him, and though Wilbur Hoyt did not approve of women joining men in their work, for he looked out at the world through a pair of pale Presbyterian eyes, he said he would see and actually smiled back at her.

She must have been an altogether adorable young woman. She was so young that Mother had had some hesitation about employing her as cook. But it turned out that she had a natural gift and learned recipes new to her very quickly, and she kept a clean kitchen. She was small, compactly built, light on her feet, with an open face, a short nose covered with freckles, and copper-brown hair which she wore in thick braids around her head. The men found her irresistible and so did I, though I suppose at aged seven I was not in a position to judge.

After the haying began, when the evenings were warm and she had put her kitchen to bed, she would take the guitar she had brought with her, sit on the lawn with her back against the trunk of the great pine that grew at the end of the farm house and sing to the farm hands and the two extra men who had come for the haying. They would sit on the grass in front of her and after a time Wilbur Hoyt would come out of his house to listen to her, and then sometimes even his wife and the wife of the teamster. Her voice carried over the noise of the brook: first songs that everybody knew, but then came the moment that I waited for as I sat on the steps of our kitchen porch.

She would put down her guitar and raise her hands to her head and her hair would come down. As she undid the braids, the hair spread over her shoulders and down her back to her hips to make a cape around her. When he first saw this happen my father, just up from New York City for his first main summer holiday, forbade me to watch any longer. I think he considered Maggie's behavior licentious. Mother expostulated in her gentle voice, but I was sent up to my room anyway. "It's way past his bed time," Father said; and in our family his word was the law.

But my bedroom window looked over the brook to the farm house and as soon as Mother had closed my door and the light of her candle had dimmed to darkness in the crack underneath it, I would steal out of bed and crouch at the window and watch Maggie singing to the men and even hear her voice. Now she sang only Irish songs, perhaps some of them in Gaelic, for I could not understand the words. Afraid that I might fall asleep and be caught at the window I would crawl back into bed.

They said that sometimes when she was done singing Maggie would stand on the bridge and look up along the brook for as much as half an hour, especially if the moon was high; but what she was looking at nobody knew and she told no one until, near mid-July, the cream started turning sour.

My father's main interest in the farm was improving his dairy herd of Holsteins. In 1910 they amounted to ninety head, not large as modern dairies go but pretty big at that time in our upstate back-country region, and they produced a lot of milk. At first this had been drawn daily to a little cheese factory at the top of Hawkinsville hill, on the far side of the canal. But father had switched to making and selling butter.

The quality of butter depends on the quality of the cream it's made from; and now suddenly our cream was turning sour before it could even leave the separator house. The butter made at Northlands had been so good that it had quickly found regular and steady customers; so good, indeed, that Father had found a buyer in his own University Club in New York City. Since he was the chairman of the House Committee there may have been a bit of nepotism (if that is the appropriate word) involved; but when two other clubs expressed an interest it looked almost as if Northlands butter might develop into (to quote Father once more) "a Famous Product." So the sudden falling off in quality became a problem of vital importance.

Of course, now and then, especially in the sultry and thundery days of August, one expected cream to go sour. But this July had been a benign month, the heat never excessive, and on the few days rain came it came without fireworks of any sort. So when the cream soured six days in a row Father became alarmed and then nearly panic stricken. At first he accused the Hoyts of being careless in their daily cleaning of the separator parts, the pans and jugs the cream sat in, the churns. But the Hoyts maintained that they had not changed in any single small detail the way in which they had always done the work. Father then instructed Mother personally to inspect their handling of the whole procedure. Mother did so, but found nothing to criticize. "Mrs. Hoyt is a terribly proud housekeeper," she reported. "Her house is so clean you can almost hear her curtains squeak."

The souring continued and Father lost all his pleasure at being on the farm. "If you can't stop this, Wilbur," he said to Mr. Hoyt, "I'll sell every damn cow on the place and you'll be out of a job."

I saw Mr. Hoyt's face freeze. He might have been about to retort, "And you'll be out of a farmer." But fortunately he did not.

Mother, who had witnessed the exchange, had swiftly gone to cover in our house, entering by the kitchen as the closest point of refuge. Maggie Corcoran was peeling carrots

29

at the kitchen sink and, hearing Mother's sigh, turned with a slight smile and said, "It would be easy to stop the cream souring, Mem."

Mother halted in midstep. "Maggie! How? You mean you know why the cream goes sour?"

"Yes, I do," Maggie answered. "It's The Other People. The fairies in the brook. When there's fairies in a brook anybody at all in the Old Country knows enough to give them their share of the cream."

"But if that's true just how do you go about giving the cream to them?" asked my mother.

"Sure, you just throw it in the water and they'll take care of it."

I think my mother may have smiled, though her back was to me, for over her shoulder I saw Maggie beaming.

"I'll tell Mr. Edmonds," Mother told her.

When she did, however, my father exploded. He had never heard such rot. It was utter nonsense. It was unseemly. It was unmoral. He would not allow such practices on any place that belonged to him. He wouldn't hear another word. "Tell that Maggie Corcoran of yours to hold her tongue," he said to Mother.

But the cream continued to sour. The two latest customers in New York—the clubs that did not have Father on their house committees—cancelled their accounts. Then Father received a letter from his own University Club asking when he expected to resume shipping butter that was up to standard. The atmosphere on he farm became excruciatingly tense. Father gave up fishing and went for long, morose walks in the woods. Day after day the cream continued relentlessly to sour.

At last, coming in from the woods late one afternoon, Father said to me in a voice that sounded strangely dead, "Run out to the barn, Watty, and tell Wilbur he may throw some cream in the brook."

I rushed out through the pantry, and finding Maggie Corcoran in the kitchen, said, "Father wants me to tell Mr. Hoyt to throw cream to the fairies. Will you come with me, Maggie?"

"All right, I will."

She caught my hand and we tore down the porch steps and over the brook towards the barn. With her free hand Maggie hiked her skirts above her knees so she could really run and I found myself being dragged rather than running on my own steam. Just the same I managed to shout, "Mr. Hoyt! Mr. Hoyt! Daddy says you can throw cream in the brook and Maggie and I are coming to help you."

Mr. Hoyt stood in the door at the end of the cattle run, a milk pail in one hand and his milking stool in the other, and I explained what I had been shouting. Perhaps it was my small boy's imagination, but I was almost sure I saw relief like a small candle far back behind his gaunt face: a light that, dim as it was, nearly brightened into pleasure.

"They're just starting to separate," he said, and as we followed him to the separator house at the other end of the barn we heard the whine of the whirring discs beginning to take voice.

"How much had we ought to give them?" he asked.

"After all this time and all the things that've been said against them, I'd throw in a gallon," cried Maggie.

"I don't think Mr. Edmonds would like to let them have that much."

"How much would he?"

"A pint, maybe?"

Maggie shook her head.

"That's not enough, after waiting this long. The Other People don't like being played with for cheap."

"A quart then," said Wilbur Hoyt, replacing the usual five gallon can with a tin quart measure.

"Full up," Maggie said firmly, watching the marvelous smooth yellow jet arcing into the measure.

"To the top," agreed Wilbur Hoyt with something like a flourish in his voice, as if responding to a toast.

He gave the full measure to Maggie, saying, "I think you are the one to do this, Maggie."

But she shook her head.

"I'll carry it down for you, but you have got to put it in the water. It's you people on the farm, Mr. Hoyt, you and the Mister himself, that The Other People feel themselves offended by."

So Mr. Hoyt poured the quart of cream into the brook and we watched it slowly curving and writhing down the current until it disappeared.

"You'll have to give them a quart every night, Mister Hoyt, for the seven days of the week, before they'll be satisfied."

"I will," he said. "I will do it, Maggie, no matter what anybody says."

Maggie smiled. The cream did not sour that night. It did not sour for the seven days of the week. It did not sour again during the rest of that summer. It left no doubt in my mind about the presence of The Other People.

But though I spent hours and days along the brook, taking my fishing rod to disguise my purpose, I was never able to see any of them. I did see things I had never seen before, nor would have seen otherwise—a hummingbird perched beside its nest, a trout in a clear pool swallowing a smaller fish, darning needles dapping the water with their tails, for what purpose I had no idea. I would sit in the shadow for half an hour at a time, but The Other People never appeared.

Five years later, however, my little sister met them. By that time I had almost forgotten about Maggie Corcoran, so when Molly appeared tardily for breakfast one morning and Mother asked her why she was late, it came almost as a shock to hear her answer that she had been kept awake for a long time by a very little man in a green coat and a tall hat, who had sat on the foot of her bed and told her stories about his people in the brook. Fortunately, Father was in New York then, for he would surely have scoffed away her story right at the beginning.

But Mother, whose sympathy, at least towards her own children, was boundless, asked, "Did he tell you what his name was?"

"Oh, yes," Molly replied. "His name was Gogie. I called him 'Mister Gogie' and he seemed to like that."

"Did he say where he came from?" Mother asked.

"I told you," Molly said, sounding slightly vexed. "He lives in the brook. He came right through the window and he stood in the moonlight before he hopped onto my bed. He had a cane like Daddy's, only it had a twist in it."

Having grown older, I had by then been moved to the third floor bedroom and my sister into my old room overlooking the brook and the bridge and the end of the farmhouse with the big pine under which Maggie Corcoran had sung to the farm hands. According to my sister the little man came back to see her two or three times; there were other times when she played along the brook that she saw him, and one or more little people like him, but none of these ever spoke to her.

I don't know whether Mother told Father about what Molly saw. I expect not, or he would have had Molly come before him in the living room for cross-examination. Besides, after that one summer Molly never again saw any of The Other People.

It would be easy to think that she made up these encounters. She was a solitary, lonely little girl—she had no playmates at Northlands—and she might easily have imagined these little people. But then there was the morning twenty-four or -five years later that my son, Peter, came down to breakfast rather late with a story about being visited the night before by a little man in a high hat who came in through the moonlight to sit on the foot of his bed and keep him awake by telling stories.

I had forgotten all about The Other People by that time. My first wife, Eleanor, assured me afterward that I had never mentioned Molly's friend or Maggie Corcoran to her; there is no reason to suppose I mentioned them to Peter, either. But here was the story again, almost in the words of my little sister Molly.

"Did this little man happen to tell you his name?" I asked.

"He did," Peter answered. "I didn't hear it very well. I guess I was pretty sleepy. But I think it was Woogie. Something like that, anyway."

So there it is.

Yet not quite all. One other member of our family very likely saw the same little man.

Our granddaughter Kate was six, I think, that summer, a good part of which she had been spending with K, my second wife, and me at Northlands. She had never said anything to us about a visitor at night, though she slept in the room that had been mine and then my sister's and Peter's; but as her mother started to drive her home to Concord at the end of her stay, Kate said, "I think I'll go to sleep now."

"Why?" her mother asked, for they were barely out of the driveway, still on the river road. "Are you so tired?"

"Yes," Kate told her. "A little man came in the window and talked a long time."

She curled on the seat beside her mother and went to sleep immediately. She did not, as far as I know, have anything more to say about her visitor. But since I have been writing all this down it has occurred to me that she may have told us something earlier in her own way. A night or two before she left, while her grandmother was getting her supper, she lay down on the kitchen floor and made a drawing of something. . . . A little man? A goblin? Possibly a bug? Here it is. You can make anything you please of it. As you can of The Other People and what Maggie Corcoran said about them.

As for me, I've often wondered. But I can never explain our summer of the sour cream.

35

Father, Walter D. Edmonds, Sr., in camp some-where on the Murray River, Quebec, 1890s. Photograph taken by himself.

Fishing with a Fly

I suppose every boy remembers getting his first fly rod. Mine came to me on July 15, 1915, my twelfth birthday. When I walked into the living room to open my presents I knew it must be in the long and narrow package, still in the brown paper that the rod maker had shipped it in. All the other packages were in birthday wrappings. Inside the paper the rod was boxed in four thin pine slats with heavier square endpieces. A screwdriver had been thoughtfully placed on the table for me to use in prying off a slat.

"Be careful how you do it, Watty," said Father. He was continually telling me to be careful.

I got the slat off with no difficulty and no damage to the box or the rod within.

"You will need the box to send the rod back in when you break it," Father observed, but I did not listen. I had lifted out the rod. Until that moment I had not been at all confident of having a fly rod of my own. When, shortly after my preceding birthday, I had announced that what I had really wanted was a fly rod. Father said I was too young and irresponsible to be entrusted with anything so fragile, but

37

after a time he had relented, I suspect at some pleading by my mother. I found it difficult to untie the tape of the snuff-brown twill envelope that encased the rod and still more difficult to withdraw the rod from the case. Fly rods in those days came packed on a sort of cylinder covered with cloth, with indented spaces to accept the two tips, the middle joint and the butt, with two tapes near the top and bottom to hold the pieces firmly in their places. I now not only held the rod, I could see it.

How can I describe it for you? The slender pieces were a pale cream color—or should I call them ivory—against more snuff-brown cloth. The windings seemed unique: a pair of black, a pair of red, a pair of black, a pair of red, all the way down to the tip end, the most beautiful rod I had ever laid eyes on. The joints of my wrists and knees seemed on the point of dissolving. I could scarcely lift the pieces from their molded places.

"Take care how you put it together," Father told me. Speechless, I could only nod. I knew how to set up a rod; I had set up his more than once when he was going off to fish. I took out a tip and the middle joint, rubbed the male end of the ferrule behind my ear for lubrication as Father had taught me (some vulgar practitioners, he said, employed the nose for this purpose) and inserted it into the female section at the top of the middle joint. They slid together with a smooth, totally satisfying firmness. I repeated the process, joining the middle joint to the butt. The handle, instead of being covered with cork, was wound with a fine gray-green cord that, to my eyes, was especially beautiful. As my fingers closed snugly around it I felt the action of the rod. I swung it gently from left to right in horizontal arcs, as I had seen Father do to "feel" a rod, and a sense of life, suddenly created, filled my being. A reel would have to be mounted and line threaded through the guides before the rod's action was complete.

There were other packages on the birthday table. From Father came a single-action reel with a line, untapered in those early days. It had a hard enamel finish that could produce all kinds of kinks and snarls if one unwarily stripped too much from the reel, but that I was yet to learn. There was a wicker creel from my mother, somewhat smaller than my father's but serviceable nonetheless, with the same sort of sling; a landing net from my brother; and a black leatherette fly book for an assortment of snelled flies and a couple of leaders from my little sister, Molly. I felt no boy could be better equipped to start out fishing with a fly. My heart burst with impatience to get off to our pond to test my skill at casting. There was, however, the birthday luncheon to sit through. On that particular morning I cared not an iota for ice cream, cake, or party crackers, but mine was not a family to permit me to slight an observance of this nature.

I shall spare you a catalog of tiresome details and give you instead the particulars of my new rod. It was seven and one-half feet long, weighed four ounces, and was made of lancewood by J. F. Pepper and Co., Inc. of Rome, N.Y. Why lancewood, not split bamboo? There were two reasons. First, lancewood was much less expensive. Behind the second reason hung a tale.

For ten or fifteen years, before, at the age of fifty, he married my mother, Father had spent each September trout fishing in Quebec, where he and a Canadian enthusiast held a lease on the Murray River, or Malbaie as it was then called. Their water began at the foot of a spectacular two hundred-foot slide called La Chute, ten or twelve miles above the river's mouth at Murray Bay, and extended all the way to the headwaters. Except for an occasional family of Indians, whose rights to fish had been retained, these two men had the river to themselves. In a real sense it was virgin fishing, and they and the friends they often took in with them came back with five- and six-pounders. Many were mounted for trophies. It was one such that a young rod maker named Pepper, about to set up business in Rome, saw in a taxidermist's shop. On impulse he sent Father one of his rods to try.

At the end of that year's fishing trip Father and two of his guides decided to make one last excursion from their base in the tiny village of St. Urbain to La Chute. It was a twenty four-mile round trip, and in their hurry to make it in the single day left to them, the head guide picked up Pepper's lancewood rod instead of the six-ounce bamboo Father had always used. The mistake was not discovered until they reached La Chute, where the four-ounce rod looked incongruously fragile against the great foaming slide, for La Chute was in spate. Yet the rod handled Father's double cast of No. 2 flies well. He sent his cast across the tumbling flood, then let it swing down with the current until his flies reached the calmer water close to shore. The minute he started to retrieve them the water exploded, he struck, and after twenty five minutes of harrowing action the head guide, wading in until he was waist deep, netted the fish. It was a silvery-gray female brook trout, twenty eight inches, 8-and-a-quarter pounds. My father never again fished with anything but a lancewood rod.

So it was unthinkable to me, too, that my rod should be anything but lancewood. Father's friends, who visited us at our house near Boonville, New York came with their costly bamboo rods made by the great rod makers of the day—Hardy in London or Leonard of New York—but none of them had ever landed an 8-and-a-quarter-pound trout, not even Mr. Corning, who had fished in nearly every country in the world.

I had thought of taking my rod up to our pond that same birthday afternoon to try it out—myself out, too, if it came to that, for Father only occasionally had allowed me to attempt a cast or two with his rod. He had suggested the pond's dam as a good place for me to practice, and I could see the sense of that, for there were no shrubs or trees to catch one's back-cast. However, when I muttered something about going up, my older brother John instantly suggested that the whole family should go with me to see how I made out. I knew I could not perform before an audience and chose instead to carry all my presents to my bedroom; I spent the rest of the afternoon taking the rod out of its case, putting it together and returning the pieces to their slots and replacing all in the envelope of twill. I did this over and over; I have no recollection of how many times, but it was a deeply satisfying afternoon.

Next day was better, because John had an appointment with the dentist in Boonville and, because my mother felt he might need an encouraging presence, she was driven over with him in the buckboard, taking Molly with her. Father was at work in the living room, finishing a brief for one of his law cases, and no one saw me when I slipped out of the house and started for the pond.

It was a heavy, gray morning without a breath of wind. The pond, with its woodland banks and small indented bays, was mysterious and hushed, the water slick and still. I put my creel and net down on the grass at the middle of the dam (I had come up with all of my accounterments), unhooked the single fly (Father had suggested I begin my efforts with only one fly on my leader), stripped some line from the reel, raised the rod tip, and began, with what has since been called all deliberate speed, my first false casts. A good deal to my surprise, the cast lengthened. I let the stripped line run free and was again surprised to see the fly shoot forward and plop into the water perhaps fifteen feet away. I retrieved the fly with short twitches as I had watched Father do, and cast again. The fly went about the same distance and hit the water with the same solid plop. I tried again, putting more force into the forward cast. I must have hurried because there was a snap at my back and the leader lighted on the pond without a fly.

There was no point in searching for the fly. Wet flies then were tied with snells; once the snell snapped or pulled free there was no remedy. But I was not unduly troubled, for I had had the foresight to begin my new way of fishing with a fly for which I had not much respect, called a Yellow Sally. Father did not think much of that pattern either. Because there were two more Yellow Sallies in the book my sister had given me, the somewhat disloyal thought entered my mind that Father had not only supplied the flies but unloaded some he considered undesirable. Still, there is no other pattern more visible in the water, so I fastened another to the leader and renewed my attempts to cast.

I shan't continue this description except to say that a magic moment arrived. I do not remember exactly when, or even how, that sudden awareness of the rod's rhythm touched my wrist and hand: the timing of the backcast, the unseen sensing of the line above and behind me, the easy curl as the forward cast began, the leader extending almost straight beyond the line, and the fly meeting the water with a touch. Once experienced, it becomes a part of the blood. It was not lost even if the excitement of an unexpected rise or too much anticipation disconbobulated the rhythm. Inevitably, it returned after a pause of a minute or two. You might call it skill, or knowledge, I suppose. To a very young fly fisherman, however, it was the beginning of life.

Every day from then on, when I got time, I went up to the pond to practice casting from the dam. My brother said that if I ever labored as hard at working as I did at fishing with a fly, I would become a famous man. I considered his remark contemptible, but Father seemed to agree with him. I ignored what they said and continued my casting. One afternoon, to my utter astonishment, a trout rose for my fly. It was a sizable fish; I even saw the red stripe on his side, and I struck with all my might. Why my rod did not break I cannot now imagine. But the leader snapped, and I lost another fly.

When I described my experience at supper I said that the trout must have weighed a pound. John laughed at me.

"It did!" I said hotly, and then remembering a phrase Mr.. Corning had used, said, "It was a real *smashing* big rise."

"Don't lie, Watty," Father said.

My mother bravely took my part.

"I don't think he's lying dear," she said. "He's just telling us how it seemed to him."

43

"It's lying all the same," Father maintained. "I don't like liars. I won't have liars in my family! Watty is always telling lies about the fish he didn't catch."

This was an accusation that could apply to fishermen other than myself, but it did not seem to me a favorable time to bring it to my family's attention, and, after all, Father could always point to the 8-and-a-quarter-pound trout *he* had caught. It was mounted under glass and hung over the living room fireplace. So I kept silent under Father's bleak stare, waiting for the subject to peter out. It did, and three days later Father surprised me by asking if I would like to go fishing with him at Miller's Hole, above us on the Black River. He had finished the brief he had been working at and could allow himself a holiday. Each of us would take his own fly rod. Surprised and feeling almost humble, I said I would like to go.

Father had left his rod mounted and resting on three pegs in the living room, but I went through my usual ritual of taking my rod out of its case and putting the pieces together on the front veranda. When I had threaded the line through the guides and tied on the leader, Father, who had been watching the deliberate process with barely disguised impatience, saw that I was hesitating over my choice of flies.

"Put on an Edmonds for the dropper and a Brown Hackle," he said. "If they don't raise a fish for you, nothing will."

The Edmonds fly had been invented accidentally by Father in his youth when, while putting a White Miller on his cast, he noticed that some red floss was caught around the body. The floss seemed hopelessly entangled, so in frustration Father used the fly as it was and immediately caught a trout on it. And then another, and another until he had six in his basket. From then on he always fished with a White Miller that had red floss around the body. He named it after himself, and by the time I came along he was having it tied by Hardy in London and William Mills and Sons in New York City. He never fished with any other pattern. He was a very consistent man in his habits. And, after all, this had paid off in that great 8-and-a-quarter-pound trout. Or so he said. There was always a picky little question in my mind because the great fish behind its bell of glass was mounted with a Brown Hackle in its jaw and the Edmonds fly below at the end of a graceful swirl of the leader.

However, after once raising the question I knew better than to do so again, and now I dutifully put on an Edmonds as my dropper with a Brown Hackle as the tail fly. We set out for our objective about half a mile upriver from the house.

We did not follow the river shore but went overland across the sand flats. Father was a vigorous walker. With my short legs I had to trot in his wake to keep reasonably close. It was a hot afternoon, even for July; my creel bumped against my knee and my landing net kept getting snagged by the scrub we passed through. I was hot and blown and tired by the time we came out above Miller's Hole. It lay fifty feet below us, a horseshoe-shaped pool, the concave shore formed by our sandy bank fully in the afternoon sun. The other shore was wooded, with a gnarled old butternut leaning far out to further shade the water.

We scrambled down to the foot of the pool and Father immediately divided the fishing. He was to keep our shore for himself because, though the sun was on it, that was where the pool was deepest, and, besides, the current from the rapids above ran along it. I could see that; now and then a grasshopper came floating down, drawing a moderate rise.

"You wade across here at the foot," Father told me, "and fish the other bank."

"I don't see anything rising over there," I said.

"That doesn't matter," Father said impatiently. "What we want is to take back a trout for Mother's breakfast, and with this sun a long cast will be needed to raise a fish. Go on, Watty. It will give you practice."

I looked up at him but could find no hint of a possible change of heart. There was nothing to do but wade to the far shore. Because the river was very low the water did not come above my waist, but I slipped and floundered on the round, uneven stones and made a good deal of splashing, which caused Father to expostulate. I paid no heed, being out of reach, and once across made my way up to the old butternut, which grew almost exactly at the apex of the convex shore. A plantation of ostrich ferns made the shade seem still cooler, and I sat down among them to nourish my resentment while I watched Father make his beautiful long casts, his backcast reaching almost as far out behind him. I despaired of ever being able to fish as beautifully as he.

There was nothing to snag his long backcasts, I observed. But how could I, only just beginning to learn the art, be expected to fish from this shore where the woods came to the water's edge? My sense of being unfairly treated swelled, and I stared across at Father with something close to real dislike. But after a few minutes subtle changes began to take place in me. I noticed that his cheek under the small white felt hat he always wore in the country was glassy with sweat. I noticed, too, that while his casts were as impressive as ever, he was getting very little action. I realized, as well, that the coolness in the ferns was even more delicious than it had been and, further, that I myself felt cool and refreshed. Beyond me the water seemed barely to move, but it was dark and green from the trees that shaded it. And all of a sudden I remembered walking in the previous autumn through the woods behind where I was now sitting and happening on a strong-running spring. Most of all I remembered following it toward the river only to see it mysteriously vanish into the ground. It went under a log but did not come up anywhere I could find, though I quartered the remaining woods between that log and the river.

Now, sitting among the ferns, the thought came to me that the spring running underground must emerge into Miller's Hole somewhere between where I sat and the old butternut. Down there where it came out the water should be a lot cooler than it was elsewhere in the pool. If I could get my fly out to wherever the cold spot was, perhaps I could find a fish.

I looked at the Edmonds fly and the Brown Hackle on my leader with skepticism and distaste. I took them off and put them back into my fly book and selected instead a fly I had seen in the local hardware store, a rather fuzzy, grayish brown affair the storekeeper called a Hare's Ear. Wading out about eight feet from shore, I tried a few horizontal casts, hoping to keep my backcast beneath the branches. It worked all right as far as that was concerned, but I could not seem to get my forward cast very far from shore. Besides, I wanted to put my fly closer to the butternut, but because it was to my right, upstream, to do so simply was not feasible. In this dilemma Mr.. Corning came to my rescue. For an old and confirmed bachelor he had a great deal of patience with a curious and persistent small boy. One afternoon he gave me a demonstration in roll casting. I was amazed at the distance he could throw a line when he had merely brought the flies in to his feet and then a sudden forward casting of the rod sent the line rolling out across the water. Mr. Corning had even let me hold the rod above his hand while he demonstrated, so I could get the feeling of what he did. He would not let me try it by myself because I wasn't strong enough to handle his Hardy rod properly.

But now I tried it with my own lancewood. And after two or three attempts I was able to get my flies ten or twelve feet out from where I stood. That, I felt pretty sure, would bring my fly over deep water.

I let my Hare's Ear drift and sink. When I though it might be deep enough, I retrieved it very slowly, giving a kind of wiggle to the top of my rod. With the next cast I moved three steps upstream. On my fourth or fifth cast I was throwing the fly into the deep shade under the butternut. And this time, as I began to bring in my fly there was a sudden, oily, utterly silent swirl in the water where I thought the fly must be. I tried not to strike too hard. But the hook went home. I had a fish on.

He felt like a pretty good one, but he did not make any great gyrations. He seemed to be bent on boring for the bottom and then towards the butternut, whose lower branches touched the water. In panic I moved downstream step-by-step until the tree was no longer a threat. Then I started backing toward the shore. The fish came along, though with considerable reluctance. But I was merciless. I kept reeling in my line, until all at once I saw a dim shape near the surface.

For the first time I remembered my landing net. Somehow it had worked its way around me till it was hanging over my rump. It was necessary to manage rod and fish with my right hand alone. I snubbed the line against the handle with my middle finger, raising the butt as high as I dared or, more probably, as I could accomplish, while I again groped clumsily behind my back for the net handle.

No matter how I tried, my fingers could not reach it. I began to grow frantic. The fish seemed to have sensed my difficulties, for he began to slop alarmingly about, this way and that near the surface. Now I could see something of it. He looked enormous, and sheer terror of his ripping himself free made me ease the pressure on the rod butt. To my relief the surface disturbance ceased and he resumed his underwater tactics. I was still unable to reach the net handle, but it suddenly occurred to me to pull on my creel sling. This brought the net's snap around enough for me to grasp it. I undid it and thrust the net out to the full stretch of my arm, dipping it underwater. Again I raised the rod butt, drawing the fish toward me. He came into the net as unprotestingly as any lamb. I lifted the net. His head was at the bottom, but what looked like a third of his length extended over the hoop. In a spasm of fright I flung fish and net together onto the bank as far as I could and followed at top speed. We fell almost as one into the ferns. I grabbed the flopping body and hammered the back of his head against a nearby stone. Then I laid him down tenderly among the ferns to hunker over him and drink in the sight of him, inch by inch and spot by spot.

I had never seen a fish exactly like him. From his red and black spots I deduced that he must be some sort of trout, but he certainly was not what in his more orotund moments Father referred to as "the noble *Salvelinus fontinalis.*" I did not know what he could be, but he was the longest trout I had seen except for specimens mounted behind glass. And *I* had caught him.

Suddenly I thought of Father and parted the ferns. He was still casting, though farther up the pool than when I had last seen him, and while I watched he raised and brought in what appeared to be a pretty small trout. He measured it, however, against the six inches marked out on the lid of his creel; the fish must have qualified for he put it into the basket. That reminded me that I should do the same with my own fish.

It was not as simple an operation as Father had experienced with his small trout. In the first place, as I have said, mine was an undersized creel. I picked a few ferns to line the bottom, not so much because ferns were supposed to help keep fish fresh and cool, but because I thought the green lining would make my trout look still more beautiful. Then I tried laying him on his bed. Of course he was much too long. I considered doubling him up on himself, but his body was too stiff to make such an abrupt curve and, besides, he would look extremely odd when I took him out after we reached home. So I compromised by bending him slightly and letting his tail emerge from the hole in the lid of the creel. The tail stuck up through the hole like the picture of the flukes of a diving whale I had often pored over in our copy of *Moby Dick.*

It was just then that Father called across the river.

"Watty, come along. There's no use fishing any longer. The sun's too bright."

I stood up among the ferns, slung the basket over my shoulder and picked up my rod and net. Just before I stepped out from the trees, however, something impelled me to hitch my basket around until it was squarely behind my back, almost hidden. Wading over, I slipped and floundered on the stones just as I had before, but Father made no comment. He just stood and watched me with impatient eyes. When I came up to him he turned abruptly and started climbing the sandy bank, and I scrabbled after him.

We walked all the way home in silence, but that did not trouble me. Inside me something was bubbling. You could not call it a song, nor yet a hallelujah. Whatever it was, satisfaction was an elemental part. The distance between Miller's Hole and home did not seem anywhere near as long as it had before.

My mother was standing on the front veranda as we walked up the drive. She had already changed for supper and, in contrast to us, looked incredibly cool and beautiful in her full white skirt and linen blouse with its stock of white piqué.

"Oh Gridgey," she said, using her pet name for Father as she looked down, "did you have good luck?"

"No," he said. "I only caught two. Almost too small to keep, but they'll make you a nice breakfast."

He opened the lid of the creel to show her, and she exclaimed over his fish, smiling in what seemed always to my eyes her heavenly way, her voice lifting as she said, "Oh

Gridgey! They're beautiful fish. Not at all small, really. I'll love them!"

The way she did this never failed to make Father glow; he didn't exactly preen himself, but you could tell how immense she had made him feel.

By then my brother and little sister had joined our group to look at Father's trout. A moment passed before my brother became aware of me.

"What did you get, Watty?" he asked. "Or did it get away?"

"Yes," my mother said, suddenly solicitous, as if realizing she had left me out. "Did you have any luck?"

"I caught a fish," I muttered. All at once I felt uncertain, as if winds might blow on me from unexpected quarters.

"Speak up," Father said impatiently.

"I said I got a fish," I repeated, quite loudly.

"Let's see him, if you did," John said.

I leaned my rod against the railing of the porch and hitched my basket around. The lid came into view with the flukes extending through the hole. Even before I unfastened the catch I sensed the hush that had gripped Father. When I nerved myself to look at him his eyes were staring at that monstrosity (as he must have thought it) of fish tail. When I opened the lid and hauled out my fish, he still was silent. So were the others until my mother, with that same lift in her voice but this time for *me*, exclaimed "Oh Watty! What a gorgeous fish! He's beautiful!"

I had straightened him out as well as I could but he still had a sort of sidewise look.

"I don't exactly know what it is," I said, "but I think it's some kind of trout."

Do you know what it is, Gridgey?" asked my mother.

Father still stared at it, distaste, contempt, and something else I was not sure of written on his face.

"I think," he said, after a moments pause, "I think it's a brown trout. A coarse kind of fish, not at all like a brook trout. Hardly worth cooking."

We looked at him. His face was flushed, his very blue eyes suddenly blazed.

"You know what Watty's fish is?" he asked us in his courtroom voice. "It's a brown trout, all right. It's a German brown trout."

Nothing he could have said could have condemned my fish more utterly. For it was now eleven months since the start of World War I. In that time Father, who was half French, had gone through many traumas, from the invasion of Belgium and France to the Battle of the Marne and, not least, changing the style of his mustache. Until August 5, 1914, he had sported a mustache with sharply upturned tips in imitation of the Kaiser, whose imperialist manners he admired. Now all things German had become anathema to him. How terrible it must have seemed to have his river invaded by a German fish! I was subdued and wanted only to take my fish away to clean it in the kitchen.

No one stopped me. Afterward I took my rod upstairs, dismantled it and wiped each piece before bestowing it in its appointed slot.

I dressed for supper. It turned out to be a rather silent meal. When it was time to go to bed my mother came out with me to the foot of the stairs.

"That's a fine fish, Watty."

"Yes," I said, speaking truth. The trout had measured sixteen-and-a-half inches and weighed a little under three pounds. "But Father thinks it was wrong for me to catch it." I added.

"Perhaps," she said. "But perhaps he thinks you were not altogether kind when you did not show it to him up there on the river."

She kissed me and I climbed the stairs, carrying a variety of thoughts which kept muzzing about until I had crawled between my sheets. I lay with hands beneath my head and caught that fish all over again. I supposed that maybe my mother was right and I had not been kind to Father. But then the suspicion came that if I had shown him the fish there by Miller's Hole he would have wanted me to put it back into the water. The more I thought of that the surer I became.

So I caught the fish in my mind still another time and at the end fell off to sleep in the sublime conviction that there was no finer sport on earth than fishing with a fly.

This picture of Mother on the edge of a field of rye is fittingly contemplative.

A Lifelong Love

I was ten years old when it first occurred to me that my mother might be in love with someone besides my father. It happened on the morning before Easter. Mother and I had just returned to our house at 18 West Eleventh Street from the French bakery at the corner of Sixth Avenue with rolls and the small dark eclairs with chocolate filling that Father was especially fond of, when the doorbell rang and Margaret, the waitress, went to answer it, returning with a large upright parcel in florist's paper, obviously a plant and obviously heavy. "Oh Mem," she said as she set it on the dining room table, "it's terrible big."

"You'd better get a plate to go under it," Mother said, "in case it's damp."

As Margaret hurried away, Mother began opening the paper. "How lovely!" she exclaimed. "Oh, here's a card."

"It's from Mr. Corning," she told me. "He shouldn't have sent such a huge one. But it *is* beautiful." Her cheeks were quite pink. She was manifestly pleased. It was a red and white azalea, trained in the shape of a tree, and perhaps thirty inches tall: the splendid kind of present I should have expected Mr. Corning to send. I admired him above all others of my father's friends.

He was a tall man, with a long and gentle face, blue-gray eyes, and a wide, naturally curving mustache. Whenever Mr. Corning came to visit us in the summer at Northlands, he brought three or four fly rods of split bamboo made by Hardy in England, and very unlike the lancewood rods my father fished with. He had used one of them when he fished the river Jordan in the Holy Land.

"What in the world made you fish in the Jordan?" my father asked with something like a snort. "Everybody knows it has no trout."

"Perhaps not," Mr. Corning replied. "I just wanted to cast a fly in the Jordan. As far as I know no one had ever done that before."

Late one afternoon he let me try my hand at casting a fly with one of his rods and when I managed to throw a respectable line he told me that it was the same rod he had had with him in the Holy Land. I returned to the house feeling proud, confident that not many boys my age had cast a fly with a rod that had fished the River Jordan. So it seemed entirely fitting that so splendid an azalea should come as a gift from Mr. Corning.

While Margaret was carrying it at Mother's instruction to a table in the living room, the telephone rang and Mother hurried to answer it. For the moment I was alone in the dining room with Mr. Corning's visiting card lying on the table in front of me. I picked it up. In his clear, almost elegant hand, above and below the embossed script of his name, he had written, "To Sally at Easter, with *all* my love."

I put it down and followed Mother into the living room, puzzled over what Mr. Corning might have meant, but feeling it was something I should not ask about. Instead, I looked again at the azalea, which seemed to me, if anything, still more beautiful. I was puzzled but it was not until my father came home that I first became troubled.

He let himself in with his latchkey and gave the special whistle that Mother and he used to call one another. (My brother and I and our little sister each had whistle calls of our own; three short notes for John, two for me, and a bobwhite for Molly.) Mother answered, whistling back, and came down the long flight of stairs, giving him a kiss and walking beside him to the living room. He, too, admired the azalea.

"What a beautiful plant! Who sent it?"

"Christopher Corning," she said.

"Wasn't there a card?" asked Father.

"Oh, yes."

"May I see it?"

"It seems to have been mislaid," Mother said. "I was looking for it just before you came home, Gridgey," she went on. "But I could not find it anywhere."

"What did it say?"

I was watching her face.

"Oh," she said, "he sent his love."

She looked composed. Her voice was perfectly serene.

Father said again, "It is a beautiful plant," and then lost interest in it. A moment later he went upstairs to change for dinner. Mother looked at me without saying anything, then followed him. And I was left alone.

I did not think the card had been mislaid and it was then I felt for the first time that she was in love with someone besides Father. I thought it must be Mr. Corning, that he and Mother must be in love with each other. I did not know why it troubled me, for I loved and admired both of them, as I loved my father also. I suppose I became upset because it did not seem orderly. From earliest childhood I liked to have everything in its proper place—the compulsion to keep things so has remained with me.

———————

That afternoon in 18 West Eleventh Street I was both right and wrong. I was right about Mr. Corning's being in love with Mother, as I would find out thirty-five years later from his niece. I was right, too, in thinking that Mother was in love with someone other than my father. But it was not Christopher Corning, though she always kept a tender place in her heart for him. It was only in 1978 that her long love was made clear to me when, in a letter replying to one of mine in which I had reiterated my feeling that Mother and Mr. Corning had been in love, my sister told me the man's name and how Mother had seen him one last time.

———————

But in those early years before the First World War whatever there might be between Mother and Mr. Corning gradually ceased worrying me. He became like one of the family, like an uncle, though much closer and more endearing than either of our actual uncles. He never forgot us three children at Christmas; most of my favorite books came from him. But it was his annual visit to Northlands that meant the most to me.

Usually he would be on his way to some fishing expedition in Maine or Canada, or to the Tahawus Club, a privately held collection of lakes and ponds along the headwaters of the Hudson River in the heart of the Adirondacks, and to my exquisite pleasure he would allow me to help unpack and arrange his fishing tackle in his bedroom. There invariably was a good deal of it: four or five rods, at least three of which would be for dry fly fishing, an art that my father, a confirmed wet fly practitioner, regarded with a good deal of condescension. "Five of them, and all made by Hardy in London," he would say. "My little lancewood made right here by Pepper in Rome wouldn't cost a quarter the price of one of yours, Christopher; but I landed my eight-pound trout with it." Mr. Corning always chuckled. "If you'd been using a dry fly, Wat, your fish might have weighed ten pounds instead of eight."

The dry flies fascinated me, so tiny, some of them, that it was hard to believe they had been tied by human hands. Perhaps, I thought, Hardy had to find young women with exceptionally clever, slender fingers to tie such perfect things, and Mr. Corning gravely agreed that that might be so. That was one of the traits that made him comfortable for a small boy to be with: he listened to what one had to say, considered it, and answered reasonably.

My brother John never took part in these proceedings. He had no interest whatever in fly fishing, except to row Father on the pond or the Black River, for which he was paid fifty cents an hour, a much higher rate than I was allowed to charge for any labor I might bring myself to perform. So from almost the beginning I saw more of Mr. Corning than he did, and in a very different light.

Always the best part of his visit, as far as I was concerned, was when he would suggest that he and I go up to the dam to try this or that rod or, still more exciting, a rod that had just come to him from Hardy's shop in London. Sitting on the side of the bed, Mr. Corning would take the rod out of its traveling case. Then he would lubricate the German silver ferrules by rubbing them on the side of his nose. He would flex the rod two or three times, after which, from a canvas carry-all bag he would pull out a reel in its leather pucker-string pouch. This brought me to my moment of importance in the ritual when, after he had fixed the reel firmly on the reel seat, he asked me to be kind enough to thread the line through the guides. Then, after the leader had been attached, came the selection of a fly. After a decision had been reached and the fly fastened to the leader with a proper turle knot, Mr. Corning would rise from the bed and ask me to get his landing net.

"We'd better take the long-handled one," he would say with a quizzical glance at my face, for he must have seen the relief I felt. Taking the long handled boat net meant that our visit to the dame would include what Mr. Corning always referred to as the liberation of the frogs.

The first dam Father had built across Crystal Creek (actually named for the original settler on the place, a crusty old German named Christol) was built by a professional engineer from Albany; but it had been breached and washed away by flood water in the following spring. Father then turned to local talent, hiring an old farmer who had built the towpaths of the Black River Feeder Canal that ran across the hillsides over the river from our place, and he built our new dam of a core of puddled clay and placed the spillway at one end; that dam still stands, though the spillway has had twice to be replaced. The first spillway was of wood and its design, according to the plan worked out by old John Kornmeyer and a Boonville carpenter, was what made necessary (in our minds, at least) the liberation of so many bullfrogs.

The spillway consisted of a level trough or raceway, twelve or fourteen feet wide and thirty-odd feet long, crossing the width of the dam, with a gently descending runway of sixty or seventy feet more, that ended in a drop of eighteen inches to the brook bed at the bottom. The raceway across the top of the dam had double walls of heavy plank, with bracing planks between every three feet or so that formed wells about five feet deep. And it was at the bottom of these wells that bullfrogs became incarcerated.

As we lay on our stomachs and peered down into these pits it was hard to see anything but a vague shadow that might or might not be a frog. But after our eyes readjusted from the sunlight, two eyes came into focus bulging up at us as, no doubt, ours bulged down at them. They provided a reference point towards which to maneuver the long-handled net. In a moment an exclamation of satisfaction would issue from Mr. Corning, deep and rich, not so unlike a bullfrog's at that: a sound I never heard him make in any other circumstance.

He would raise the net straight up out of the well, one hand alternating below the other on the handle, until the net itself appeared with its load of froggy corpulence, eyes bulging more than ever as he regarded our faces through the mesh. How or what had caused it to fall into the well no one could imagine, but it was plain that plenty of grasshoppers, slugs, and other insects must have fallen in too, for by midsummer many of these specimens were big beyond belief. In any case, with Mr. Corning holding the net above the raceway, we would crawl to a point opposite where the horizontal flooring gave way to the long slope.

Over the years the planks had grown a skin of mossy slime, green and forty times more slippery than ice. Once free of the net there was no way the frog could find traction for jumping. Even if he could have he was hemmed in by the wooden sidewalls. He was helpless to go anywhere but down the long incline. With the low midsummer flow there would be no more than three or four inches of water, so the frog's descent was slow and mostly dignified. He might scrabble but usually he accepted the inevitable, revolving deliberately so that his bulging eyes stared now at us, where we lay convulsed with laughter, now at the inevitable culmination of his descent to the mild white water at the apron's end, into which he would tumble, legs showing impossibly long and thin above the froth, and then to swim with leisurely strokes down the pool to safety, while Mr. Corning and I went back to perform another liberation.

———

After these shared exercises in rescuing frogs it was impossible to feel any uneasiness about Mr. Corning; I accepted and trusted him without reserve. My brother sometimes joined in our frog liberation sessions and enjoyed them as much as we did, but he never had the close relationship with Mr. Corning that I had, a relationship that became closer as the years went by.

This culminated in 1920, when it was decided that Mother needed relief from managing the household at Northlands and we spent two months at the Tahawus Club of which Father, as well as Mr. Corning, was a member. The mountain lakes within the boundaries of the club property held bass or trout, and fishing, naturally, preoccupied the membership. Of the lakes far enough from the main clubhouse to necessitate cabins of their own, Lake Colden, with its neighboring Lake Avalanche and the Flowed Lands, offered so much the best fishing and was so sought after that a member's stay was limited to five days.

Mr. Corning had made a reservation for the end of July, intending to take a friend in with him. But when the friend at the last minute was unable to come, I was invited in his place, "if Wat would care to come." As if there could be any question. My father was in New York at the time, but Mother saw no reason why I should not accept.

So for five days, except for the hours spent fishing, we were alone together and I came to know a great deal about him that I hadn't known before. He was a mining engineer whose profession had taken him to all parts of the world: Eastern Europe, the Middle East, South Africa, North and South America, the Far East. He had been one of the first Americans, if not the first, to cross the Gobi Desert. And as I said, he had cast a fly in the River Jordan. And all these things he told me in his quiet, gentle voice, as if he spoke of every day occurrences. And at the same time simple things enlisted his complete attention: the tiny parade of Grenadier moss through a bar of sunlight along the side of a log; the call of a thrush near dusk; the fall of water in a mountain spring. He taught me to see and to listen. And when one afternoon I returned to our cabin with a better than two-pound trout, he was elated, predicting it would be the club's high hook in what was a meager fishing season. He was proved right.

As it turned out we had five additional days at Colden because the next man due to have the camp was unable to come and suggested that Mr. Corning stay on in his place. My father, who by then had returned from the city, was outraged that a seventeen-year-old boy should have had so much time on the club's best lakes, but I regretted not a moment of it.

Four winters later, when I was home from college, Mr. Corning asked if I would come to see him in his rooms at the old Murray Hill Hotel. I found him in bed, propped up against a mass of pillows, pale and strangely weak, but perfectly clear in his mind and with the same kindness in his eyes. For a while he talked about our time together at Lake Colden and those earlier visits to Northlands, especially about our liberation of the frogs. But then he wanted to know how things went with me at Harvard. I told him a little about my courses and more about writing stories for the *Advocate,* the under-graduate literary magazine; and I mentioned that my father disapproved of the kind of stories I had had published. Mr. Corning considered that with his old seriousness, then he said I should listen to what my father had to say, but then to go on with what I thought I ought to do, in my own way.

"But Wat," he added, "you should seriously think of writing detective stories, mysteries. That's where the real money lies for an author."

Mainly to please him I said I would, but the production of mystery stories remained as alien to me as the career in chemical engineering my father wanted me to pursue.

Mr. Corning had fallen back against his pillows, with his eyes closed, but in a moment they opened.

"Give my love to all your family, Wat. And especially to your mother." Then as if to himself he said her name: "Sally." His eyes closed. Suddenly he was very tired, and said good-bye. I did not see him again. He moved to Litchfield, Connecticut, where he had bought a place, and lived alone until his death. But thirty-four or -five years later his final word came back to me when one of his nieces said, "Oh, yes, all of us knew that Uncle Christopher was in love with Sally May Edmonds. Over and over we heard him say he had never met another woman like her. But of course it was impossible for him to marry her, so he would never marry anyone else. We all felt how terribly sad it was. Do you think your mother knew?"

In answered that I could not say. I thought she must have known, or at least suspected. I said she was very fond of Mr. Corning and admired him. But in the end I could not really tell. I had no way at that time of knowing that all along she had loved another man, had loved him since she was twenty or twenty-one.

I do not know when my mother met Frank Crowninshield for the first time. I should guess that it was not too long after 1890, when she turned twenty. In any case they had known each other for some time before she first met my father in 1899. Mother had also been "interested," as it was said in those days, in Francis Rogers, and the "interest" seems to have been mutual. But Rogers had embarked on an uncertain career as a singer and had very little money, and Mother felt that she could not in fairness encourage him. But she felt very differently towards Frank Crowninshield, who was even more impecunious. She was *really* in love with him, according to my sister, and did her best to encourage *him*, but he never mustered the nerve to propose to her. If she had had money of her own she might have had him, impecunious or not; but her father, Joseph May, was minister of the First Unitarian Church in Philadelphia and himself the son of a minister, and the ministry, especially when pursued through successive generations, is not a calling conducive to the accumulation of wealth. So she was left with no recourse. The years passed and by 1899 she was on the verge of becoming thirty, an age which to matchmaking relatives was a cause of increasing concern and to my mother, I expect, no less than to others. But then she met my father.

She had gone to New York to visit her uncle Eastman Johnson, a portrait painter of distinction, and his wife Bessie in their house on Gramercy Park. Her mother had died while Sarah was still a child and Uncle Eastman had always shown special fondness for her. On this visit he and Aunt Bessie had planned a dinner-theater party with another couple and a young bachelor friend whom they considered attractive and highly eligible. But alas (or not, depending on one's point of view), this paragon at the last moment was unable to come, so they turned to Walter Edmonds, also single, also attractive, and also highly eligible, and he accepted.

The play they went to was "The Merchant of Venice," and Father (as he was to become) sitting next to her, was astonished and overcome when he saw "her bosom heave" (to use his own words when he told my sister long, long afterwards) with sympathy *for Shylock!* From then on, added my sister, he was hooked, and, she still further added, it *was* a lovely bosom!

At times my father would have difficulties in reaching a decision, but now his only doubt (as he was to write Joseph May) was whether he "was worthy" of so peerless and beautiful a young woman. But the doubt seems to have had no effect in slowing the pace at which he pursued his purpose. In the end he did take one precaution in order to assess her true worth. He invited her to go into the Canadian woods for three weeks of trout fishing up the Murray River, the exclusive rights to which he and a Canadian sportsman, George Blake, leased from the Quebec government. It would be entirely proper, he explained to the Reverend Joseph May, because his friends, the Honorable Peter Barlow, a judge of the New York Municipal Court, and his wife, Louise, had already accepted and would act as chaperones. Mother accepted without hesitation and Joseph May made no demur.

The expedition was a huge success. Peter Barlow was a jolly, large, almost corpulent individual who kept everyone in good spirits, and his pretty, high-spirited wife, considerably younger than her husband, took pains to assure Mother that a difference in age was not what mattered in marriage. Then Mother soon found she liked less to cast a fly than to ride in Father's canoe and watch *him* fish, which suited him down to the ground. Altogether, by the time they had returned to Philadelphia, if Father had had even the shadow of a doubt along the way, it had long been dispelled by a veritable Borealis of emotional fervor. Nothing remained except to summon his resolve to propose to her. As he stood in the front door to say good-bye, he told her that he had a letter in his pocket which he didn't know if he had the courage to mail.

Without hesitation Mother told him to leave the letter with her. He took it from his pocket and placed it in the bowl of visiting cards on the hall table. The maid announced the arrival of his cab. He said good-bye and rushed away to catch the New York train. When he reached his bachelor apartment on Union Square, he found a telegram. It contained a single word: YES.

In due course announcements of the engagement of Sarah May to Walter Dumaux Edmonds went out and, since there could be no mother of the bride, Mother's older sister Lucretia Kay Wintersteen—Aunt Lucree to us children when we took our places in the family pattern—assumed entire charge of the proceedings. She was ash blonde, vivacious, gay, warm-hearted, and utterly unable to stop talking. Purely for their own good she tried to direct the life of every being who came in contact with her. Now she snatched her sister from their father's house and brought her to her own, where she could supervise all prenuptial activities, including the selection of Mother's trousseau. Indeed, the marriage itself would take place in the Wintersteen house.

The first congratulatory letters began to arrive, among them one from Francis Rogers, the young singer, which was generous and tender. As the letters mounted in number, Lucretia remarked that it seemed strange Frank Crowninshield had not written. Mother replied that he was not by inclination a letter writer, which Aunt Lucree thought strange in a man who expected to make a career in writing. Mother became pensive, Lucretia reported, whenever Frank Crowninshield's name was mentioned, and she was relieved whenever my father came down from New York for a brief Sunday visit. The wedding date was fixed for February twenty-second and invitations were mailed.

Wedding presents began to arrive. The family was surprised by their number, especially the Reverend Joseph May, who looked at every card.

"I believe every member of the parish has sent a gift!" he exclaimed. "I can't understand why they should have done so."

"Because they regard you as a saint and love you, Papa," Lucretia said, which was true.

Though no one ever called any of his sermons inspiring, they were regarded as earnest and instructive. I have found them difficult to read. One of his nephews, Valentine May, once said to me that he never counted sheep when trying to win sleep; he just picked up his book of Uncle Joe's sermons and opened it at random.

Everything proceeded smoothly until late one afternoon in mid-December when Lucretia, returning from another round of shopping, found the housemaid hovering anxiously in the front hall.

"I don' think Mis' Sarah well, Mis' Wintersteen. She all weepy. I think you best go see her."

"Why? Did anything happen?" Lucretia asked.

A gentleman had called. He didn't give his name, "Just say it's Frank."

My mother had come down and joined him in the front parlor, closing the door into the hall. He had not stayed long. The maid had heard his voice. Not Miss May's. And he had let himself out.

Lucretia found her sister in tears, alone in her bedroom. She had obviously experienced an emotional shock. She looked up and said something about not knowing what to do. About not being fair to Walter Edmonds if she married him. Lucretia was so alarmed that she sent for the family doctor, begging him to come immediately. He talked quietly to my mother as he took her pulse, listened to her heart with his ear pressed against her chest. Eventually he came out of the bedroom and told Lucretia that her sister was on the edge of a nervous breakdown. He prescribed absolute quiet and rest. She was to see no one except the immediate family. "Not even her fiancé?" asked Lucretia. Not even he, the doctor said.

For nearly six weeks Mother lived in solitude. Lucretia had to explain to Father, when he came down from New York in spite of her warning telegram, that he would not be able to see his Sarah for some time. He accepted the situation and asked only, in a strained voice, if it would help Sarah if they broke off their engagement, but Lucretia said decidedly, "No!" She was determined that Sarah would be married.

At the end of six weeks she told her sister that she would have to face up. Mr. Edmonds was a splendid man, the most dynamic that had ever come into Sarah's life. She would be a fool not to marry him.

Suddenly my mother seemed to come to herself. The wedding took place as scheduled, on February twenty-second. The couple departed on their honeymoon in South Carolina. And their first son, my brother John, was born exactly nine months and six days later.

Not bad, considering that groom and bride were ages fifty and thirty.

As far as I know my mother never afterwards laid eyes on Frank Crowninshield until a few months before her death. If he saw her in all those years, he certainly did not approach her, but honored his angry vow never to speak to her again. Walter and Sarah Edmonds set up housekeeping first in his apartment on Union Square, next in a rented house on lower Second Avenue, and finally in the old Federal house, which Father bought, at 18 West Eleventh Street, in which he died on April 30, 1924.

After his death she and my sister moved into the first of three apartments on the upper East Side, in the third of which my mother did encounter Frank Crowninshield for one last time. For several years she had suffered from acute angina, often bedridden for weeks at a time. But in that last year, for a while she seemed to get much better, well enough now and then even to leave the apartment for a short walk, once even for a little shopping. It was during this period of remission that she learned from the building superintendent that one of the apartments below her floor had been bought by a Mr. Frank Crowninshield. "You know, Mrs. Edmonds. The editor of *Vanity Fair*," he said with pride.

A few days after that, accompanied by her trained nurse, Mother went out for one of her little walks up and down the block. As she stepped from the elevator a man came through the front door. They passed each other in the lobby, only feet apart. I expect my mother inclined her head in her characteristic little bow, no doubt murmuring his name as she was wont to do when spotting an acquaintance though he or she might be on the far side of a street crowded and clamorous with traffic. In the quiet of the lobby Crowninshield must have heard the murmur. Her certainly could not have failed to see her, but he gave no sign of recognition.

In her letter to me my sister wrote, "Either before of after that near encounter Mother found a piece of Crowninshield's about old age and how awful it was to suddenly confront what once had been a beautiful girl and was now a travesty. I *think* he included himself in this crack-down—but he gave no quarter to growing old. So they never met again. He died before she did."

And then my sister Molly ended her letter, as well as the affair:

"Above all, I remember her quiet announcement to me that Frank C. had come there to live—a silent, ageless, sad intensity."

*My brother, John, holding Commodore, with me
on top (for the moment).*

Born to Be Hanged

"W hy do you sign your name like that, Daddy?" I asked.

It was the first Sunday morning in the month and, as was his usual practice, my father was drawing checks to pay household bills—except, that is, those from the grocer, the butcher, and the fish market. Food was the province of my mother. For this my father gave her a monthly allowance, and any expense in excess of that amount was apt to produce a term of apprehension and tension that seemed to affect the entire ménage.

"What do you mean by that?" asked my father, an immediate edge of impatience in his voice.

"Those loops on top," I said. "The one from the *D* that goes left and the one from the *E* that goes right.

I leaned against the rim of his desk to get a closer look while my father drew back in his chair and stared down at his signature with somewhat the air of a connoisseur who reappraises a work of art.

"I don't see anything wrong with those loops. They balance each other," he said.

"Is that why you make the *S* go up so high at the end? Like the tail of a frisky heifer?" I asked.

"Don't be coarse, Watty. But the *S* balances the capital *W* at the front, don't you see? Not many men have a signature like mine, as a matter of fact." There was a note of complacence in his voice, perhaps even of self-approval. "It would be impossible for anyone to forge my signature."

"What does 'forge' mean?" I asked.

"Well. Imitate. When somebody imitates another man's signature and writes it on a check for a sum of money and then cashes that check at a bank, that's committing forgery. Which is something, Watty," he added in tones of great severity, "no honest person would even *dream* of doing."

His emphasis was lost on me.

"I don't see why it would be so hard to imitate your signature." I became aware of change in the rhythm of his breathing but remained heedless, leaning still harder against the rim of the desk to examine the signature at the closest possible range.

The desk was a replica of the one George Washington had used at Mount Vernon. My father had a penchant for associating himself with great figures of history or literature. At Northlands, the name he had given our farm in upstate New York, he would often, as we walked back up the drive from the mailbox on the river road, look ahead to the gray clapboard house with its white verandah pillars and quote Thomas Babington Macaulay:

> But he saw on Palatinus
>   The white porch of his home;
> And he spake to the noble river
>   That rolls by the towers of Rome.

> "O Tiber! Father Tiber!
>   To whom the Romans pray,
> A Roman's life, a Roman's arms,
>   Take thou in charge this day!"

The fact that the river at our backs was the merest trickle in summer, because of the water taken from it by the feeder for the Erie Canal, or that the turned wooden pillars on our porch were hollow, as to his annoyance I liked to demonstrate by thumping them with my hammer or a stone, meant nothing to Father, whose spirit soared at the merest thought of heroic conduct. There were times when he must have found my older brother, my younger sister, and me difficult if not incomprehensible, and his role as our father a heroic one. Horatius and George Washington had also faced fearful odds.

Perhaps I should have sensed that I was entering on dangerous ground, but I was bored as I always was after our return from the country. There I centered my life on the working of the farm or else spent hours alone in the woods. New York City held nothing to interest me, and Sundays were by far the dullest days of the week. At eleven, moreover, one's intuitions are more inwardly directed. In my father's signature I had discovered something of absorbing interest. I pressed ahead.

"Signing your name in that complicated way ought to make it easier to imitate, not harder," I announced, watching the motions left and right as he signed still another check.

"You think so, do you?" His voice was loaded with exasperation. For an instant his hand faltered, but immediately resumed control and completed the check without a hesitant line.

Father wrote a backhand script. He held the penholder, with its Falcon nib, between the first and second fingers of his right hand. It looked a very awkward way to go about the business of putting thought to paper, but he wrote with great rapidity. In fact all his briefs were drafted by his own hand in stylograph books and he had developed his backhand style two or three years after beginning the practice of law in 1876, working for the firm of Anderson and Young at a salary of twenty dollars a month.

I don't know whether the firm employed any women. Probably not, because six years earlier there had been only seven women stenographers in the entire country. Nor was it likely that there were any typewriters in that office. An American patent had been taken out in 1868, but it was not until 1881 that Messrs. Sholes and Glidden took their invention to E. Remington and Sons in Ilion, New York, and the first practical typewriters were manufactured. At Anderson and Young every document was written out and copied in longhand and undoubtedly this endless drudgery fell upon the younger employees. Writer's cramp became almost a universal ailment and, to alleviate his, my father adopted his unusual manner of holding his pen and abandoned what had been a clear Spencerian hand for his backhand style of writing.

He had come a long way from the office of Anderson and Young to his present standing as one of the country's two top specialists in the practice of patent law, to this Federal row house at 18 west Eleventh Street and the thousand acre summer place upstate, a progress of which he not infrequently reminded me but in the course of which the angularity and near-illegibility of his handwriting had been only reinforced.

I watched him write another check, this time for O. Unti, the Italian tailor at the Sixth Avenue end of our block who pressed his clothes and did occasional alterations. In my eagerness not to miss the smallest motion made by his pen I must have pressed too close, for his hand jerked and a blob of ink flew from the nib and defaced the check for Mr. Unti.

"God damn it, Watty!" Father shouted. "See what you've done. This check is ruined."

I instantly recoiled. Though my father was a passionate man with a flashing temper, I had only once before heard him utter a word of profanity. But I was not unduly cast down. His check book was a large one with what seemed to me plenty of unused checks still left in it. Mr. Unti need not suffer; and I watched alertly as Father tore the check from the book and then in two and dropped it into the wastebasket.

"You know perfectly well that you're not supposed to come into the library when I am busy," he said. "Go upstairs. You must have homework to do."

"I've done it," I said, with a certain amount of truth.

"Go anyway. You've bothered me enough."

I went, but with the resolve to return as soon as he left the library, for I had seen that when he had torn Mr. Unti's check in two, his signature had remained intact. I wanted that signature.

I am not sure whether at that moment I had formulated a plan for its use. Retrieving it from the wastebasket filled my mind with an obsessive force and when, not long after I had reached my third floor bedroom, Father called up the stairs to put on my overcoat and cap and join him in a Sunday walk, I was suddenly terrified that Alice, the new waitress, in her eagerness to make a favorable impression, might slip into the library while we were out and empty the wastebasket.

But there was no way I could refuse Father, whose invitations at that early stage of my life amounted to commands. I got into my stiff blue cheviot coat, which I disliked, picked up my cap, and descended to the front hall where Father waited for me. It being a cold November morning, he was wearing one of the coaching coats made for him by a London tailor. It was of sand-colored whipcord, cut much longer than the ordinary overcoat, and had a cape. In it, with the pearl gray Fedora which he wore at a precise, slight tilt over his right eye, my father cut a figure on Fifth Avenue. To my embarrassment people would turn to look at him as we walked past, but he evidently relished their attention, as one could tell by the extra flourish with which he swung his cane.

Briskly turning the corner out of Eleventh Street, we started up the avenue. It was a bright, exhilarating day, at least so Father kept assuring me. But he got small response, for to me any day spent in New York City was a day wasted from my life, and all I looked forward to was the morning in early May when the family—parents, children, maids, and my brother's two canaries—left our house at precisely seven-thirty in two hired cabs, bound for Grand Central Station where the Empire State Express waited to transport us upstate for our long summer on the farm. On this cold

November Sunday, however, that morning seemed dismally far off. I walked glumly beside Father, not listening to his comments, often pointed, about the clubs or private houses along our way and the people who inhabited them.

At Twenty-third Street we turned back, though not before Father had taken time to admire the tower of Madison Square Garden, which he considered the most beautiful in New York, and especially the golden statue of Diana that crowned it. Half French as he was, the fact that St. Gaudens had been directly inspired by Houdon's *Diana* at the Louvre served only to increase his admiration.

I shuffled my feet in combined impatience and anxiety, wondering how long it would be before we got home, having, at eleven, small confidence in my own continence. Mercifully, this time my father did not commune with the goddess unduly. In only a few minutes we were on our way, and I even began to take some interest in the passing traffic. Motor coaches were beginning to supplant the horse-drawn omnibuses. From time to time a private automobile stuttered by. Even a motorized hearse appeared and I started to remove my cap to stand at attention as Father had taught my brother and me to do, rapping our heads sharply with his cane if we were slow to bare them. But to my surprise he paid no attention to the motor hearse and the thought flitted through my head that it was the netted horses and plumed vehicle that he respected more than the sad body on its final drive. As the years went by, also, it became obvious to us all that Father's affinity for the internal combustion engine was almost nonexistent.

In any case, there on Fifth Avenue, I was only too happy to get on with our return to the house. For once, my mind preoccupied with the fate of the torn check, I was able to make my short legs match his pace and as soon as Father had gone upstairs to get ready for lunch, I scurried into the library, where I found that my apprehensions about Alice's zeal were unfounded. The check was there, the signature intact as I had supposed. And I was soon to learn that Alice relied more on her highly personable looks and manner to create a favorable impression than on any meticulous performance of what used to be called her duties.

I put the check into my overcoat pocket, taking care not to wrinkle it in any way, and went upstairs. Father emerged from his predinner ablutions in the bathroom as I hurried along the landing to the foot of the second flight. He took no notice of my passage. I made it safely to my third floor bedroom. It remained to find a suitable repository for the purloined signature. I had given this problem a good deal of thought during our walk home. The small table that served me for a desk had only a single, very shallow drawer. Plainly, it would not do. Beside the table my room contained only a chair, a narrow brass bed, and my bureau. The floor was covered with dark brown battleship linoleum, the edge of which could nowhere be lifted. As far as I could see, I would have to find my safe deposit in the bureau.

I had concentrated on that while we walked the last three blocks from Fourteenth Street. Concealing Father's signature under shirts, underwear, or nightgowns would be no good at all because under strict enjoinders from my mother, the housemaid unvaryingly put any clean garment at the bottom of its appropriate pile. Even handkerchiefs were treated so. And if I kept it in the middle of any pile, it would soon become wrinkled or otherwise messed up.

But as we were passing the brownstone Presbyterian church that filled the block front between Twelfth and Eleventh Streets, I suddenly thought of a safe hiding place. This was to pull the top drawer of the bureau entirely out and to fasten an envelope to its back. In the envelope the signature would remain safe and unmussed.

In those days there were no thumbtacks, but I had a bottle of glue and with it I stuck a thick white envelope to the back of the drawer. After waiting a few minutes to make sure the envelope would not come off I put father's signature inside and replaced the drawer. Two flights below I heard the gong being stroked by Alice to announce Sunday dinner. I hurried to our third floor bathroom, passed my hands swiftly through the water gushing from the tap, and went down to join the family at the dinner table.

It was an auspicious meal. All of the dishes were ones I liked best, even the dessert. We three children considered Father's preferences—which ran to items like tapioca pudding and custards of various kinds—deplorable. But on this Sunday we had vanilla ice cream—ice cream was always made at home with an old fashioned dasher—and chocolate sauce. I returned to my bedroom as soon as seemed reasonable, with reinforced confidence in my ability to forge my father's signature.

I was quickly disillusioned. Having locked my door, taken off my jacket and hung it in the closet, rolled up the sleeves of my Sunday shirt to keep the cuffs clean, I sat down at my table and made my first attempt. My unformed hand simply could not reproduce the bold, slashing strokes with which my father signed his name. I tried again. If anything my pencil wobbled worse. But I kept on trying. I must have scrawled fifty attempts at that signature, none any good, before at length I sat back and really assayed my efforts. There was no question; I was getting nowhere. I even began to smell defeat. But I would not accept that. There had to be a way to train my hand.

I became aware that it ached. Perhaps, it seemed to me, I was getting the writer's cramp which had caused my father to hold his pen between his second and third fingers and therefore adopt his backhand style. Now I realized that in my eagerness for quick success I had been holding my pencil in the normal fashion. Naturally I could not expect to reproduce his backward slant in that way. Flushed with renewed hope I took the pencil between my second and third fingers and had another go.

This time the first four strokes that made up Father's W seemed easier. It was not yet by any means identical, but to my eyes there was a considerable resemblance. However, when I tried to carry it forward into the next letter my pencil seemed to lose its way. To reassure myself I did more Ws and thought I saw improvement.

After a while, it occurred to me that I should master each letter separately before even thinking of writing them off in brilliant sequence. So I tried to form Father's *a* and found it easier to imitate with reasonable accuracy than the W. With a dozen more samples of each letter on my pad, I sat back again to take stock. Obviously this mastering of one letter at a time would take a good deal longer than I had counted on. There were fourteen of them, and I foresaw that the capital *D* would be the most critical of all—it was, so to speak, the keystone of the signature. Someone a while before had explained how dropping the keystone of an arch into place was crucial to the whole construction. I had a set of European building blocks of red and blue and yellow stone in various shapes with which I had been able to demonstrate this for myself. It had been a rather tricky procedure and, staring at Father's signature, it was clear to me that fitting in the capital *D* would be the same.

I realized suddenly that time was getting on. I had no idea how late it was; there was no clock to tell me and I had no watch. My brother had been given an Ingersoll the year before and, though I had been told I would get one this coming Christmas, I resented the fact that he was privileged and I was not. Now, however, that was beside the point. I saw that it would be unwise to spend so much time in my room that people would wonder what I was up to. I restored Father's signature to its envelope at the back of my bureau drawer and tore my efforts at forgery into as small pieces as I could. When I opened my door at last my small sister was waiting for me in the upstairs hall with the announcement that Father had gone to his club and Mother expected us three children to join her at tea in her bedroom. It was a time all of us enjoyed.

Refreshed by tea suitably diluted with nearly the same amount of milk, and cinnamon toast, I should have liked to return to my clandestine enterprise, but that was impossible. I would need light, and I was not permitted to light the gas lamp by myself. Tomorrow there was school.

My brother and I went to a private day school on the upper East side, on East Sixty-third Street, if I remember.

This meant leaving the house before eight o'clock, walking the length of Eleventh Street, then up three blocks to the Fourteenth Street station of the Sixth Avenue Elevated, riding to Fifty-ninth Street, and then walking again, three crosstown blocks and four to the north. It seemed to me an excessively long way to go for an education. All that could be said in its favor was that the trip home in the early afternoon seemed shorter. Then, with school safely behind me, I could check the advertisements in the elevated cars or the billboards on the roofs of buildings. Some came to seem almost like friends: Ed Pinaud, with his pointy mustache and his essences for fastidious barbershop customers; the sleepy boy in his nightgown who advertised Kelley tires with the slogan "time to retire"; the Phoebe Snow whom I, along with assorted other American males, thought extremely beautiful, and who always took the Lackawanna "Road of Anthracite" to protect her clothes of unblemished white from cinder smudges. To me they had become real people and though my brother, being older, scoffed at the idea, I had persisted in so regarding them. But my mind was entirely absorbed by my program to duplicate my father's signature.

As we came down the steps from the Fourteenth Street station and our train went rattling off above our heads, I told my brother that I had to stop at Mr. Aspinwall's. He said if I did I'd have to walk the rest of the way alone, but that did not bother me. The Ninth Avenue boys almost never showed up in our district on week days until the end of the afternoon and usually made trouble only if you were on or carrying roller-bearing skates. So we parted and I entered Aspinwall's by myself.

One side of the shop was devoted to stationery. The other side displayed what, in the country, were called "notions," all sorts of useful items for stuffing out Mother's Christmas stocking. The far end was devoted to cards for Christmas, Valentine's Day, Easter, and other occasions of health or the lack of it. My present interests lay in stationery.

I had nearly used up my ruled pad the day before. I needed several more, but budgeting my available change, I settled for two. With them I asked for two pencils, medium lead. Usually I preferred soft pencils for the very black lines they produced. But soft pencils, in the marathon process ahead of me, I now realized were impractical. I would probably use one up every two or three days. With these purchases in my bag and the proper funds paid over to Mr. Aspinwall, I was ready to leave.

"I trust those medium pencils will prove satisfactory," he said, surprisingly, for he was a tactful little man who allowed children to make their choices by themselves and take as much time doing so as they wanted.

"Oh, I think so," I said and felt myself flush. Being well aware of the questionable aspects of the course I was embarked on, I was in constant fear of someone else's divining my plan. But at once, looking up at Mr. Aspinwall's gentle and very correct face, I was at ease again. He could not possibly know.

Once at home, and safe again behind my locked door, I resumed operations, pursuing my objective of mastering each letter separately. I used up my original pad and began on one of the new ones. It, too, was half used up when fading daylight brought me to a stop. I had four letters by then that looked to me reasonably like the original: W *a l t*. In a moment of recklessness, if not abandon, I tried them quickly in sequence and had a "Walt" that in my eyes looked better than the separate letters. Elated, I put everything back in place and went downstairs.

"We didn't wait tea for you, Watty," my mother said. "Were you doing your homework?"

"No," I replied. "Not exactly."

My brother, John, snorted. "Not exactly! What *were* you doing?"

I searched my mind hurriedly for something that might not be too far from truth.

"Well," I said. "I was doing some kind of a story."

"A story," my mother said, approvingly. The only thing in school I seemed to be good at was writing very short stories, mostly based on the animal life of the farm, for my English class. "When can we see it?" Mother asked.

"It's longer than I thought it was going to be," I told her, now coming closer to the truth. "It's going to take quite a long time."

"It will be fun to see it when it's done," Mother said. But on that point I felt some doubt; I hadn't the faintest idea of what would happen. What was more important: I did not know whether it would actually get done at all.

If I had put one-tenth of the energy and concentration into my school work that winter that I lavished on my effort to forge Father's signature, I might have equalled if not excelled my brother's marks, which almost never fell below ninety, and in doing so, rejoiced my parents' hearts. But I did not. I even lost my enthusiasm for writing stories.

Christmas came and went. I got my Ingersoll watch, and in that at least I was now as good as John. My entire being was dedicated to my illicit purpose. When at New Year's dinner I refused to eat creamed celery, which I despised, and was sent up to my room "to think things over," I lost not a moment in assembling my paraphernalia and going to work on the forgery. Even when the waitress, Alice, brought a plate of the ice cream dessert to my room in sympathy, I resented her intrusion, repeating to myself Father's favorite saw that "Hell is paved with good intentions." I managed, however, to eat the ice cream.

So the weeks went by. Looking back on the long-ago winter, I find it difficult to understand the compulsion that enabled me to persevere in the face of such painfully slow progress. By February, I had worked over all fourteen letters and could decently reproduce them singly, or even in threes or fours. But whenever I tried to dash off the whole signature with its loops and flourishes, my hand collapsed.

My premonition had been right. It was the capital *D* that broke my rhythm, and the most difficult thing about it was the line that began as the cross of the *T* in Walter and ended to begin the downstroke of the capital *D*. The *D*, also, was difficult, with its savage strokes. It looked fierce to me, the kind of fierceness you meet in the eyes of a bull staring into your own eyes between the bars of his pen. It was almost as if Father disliked the *D* and had to get it over. I began to think that *D* was going to beat me, because there was something about my hand that rendered it incapable of forming a letter of such passion. It became obvious that I needed some way to help me beat the *D*.

And then near the end of February, two things happened to get me over the hurdle. The first was my own doing. I had stopped in at Aspinwall's again, on my way home from school, to make my customary purchase of pencils and ruled pads. The counter was out of my kind of pad and Mr. Aspinwall went off through the green curtains at the back of the store for a fresh supply. While he was gone, I picked up another pad and lifted the cover. The paper was slick, almost waxy, and when Mr. Aspinwall returned, I asked him what the pad was for.

"Tracing paper," he said. And of course I knew, or should have known, for in a way it was like the stylographic pads on which Father wrote his briefs in longhand. I had just enough change to pay for it as well as my usual items.

As soon as I could get to my room, I put Father's signature under the top sheet of tracing paper and saw with delight that it showed through clearly. So I began to make a series of tracings. Having earlier mastered the individual letters, I found that I could follow the actual outline almost automatically. The tracing paper helped also to gain a feeling for Father's swooping loops. Only at the capital *D* was the going difficult. Even in tracing it, I could see uncertainty in the track my pencil left. I kept working at it and working at it until I had used up the first pad of tracing paper and was well into a second.

Then one afternoon Mother said that she would have a special treat for us at tea. When we three children had gathered in her bedroom and had all had our first cup, Mother picked up a little green booklet, bound by a ribbon through holes in the folds of its pages.

92

"This," she said, "is the little recollection your French grandmother wrote not long before she died, about her coming to America and finally to Utica where she met and married your grandfather and where Daddy and his sister were brought up. I think it's going to interest you."

It did. It told about our grandmother as a girl, sailing for America with her younger brother, and how their ship survived a storm so terrible that it was barely able to make port in the Azores and had to spend three weeks at anchor before it was made seaworthy once more. After that her little story was less exciting, though it was satisfying to learn how she finally came to Utica so that our father could get born. When Mother put the book down I asked if I might see it. Grandmother's name was on the cover—Eugénie Doumaux Edmonds. I stared at it for a full minute.

"Grandmother spells her name D-O-U," I pointed out, "and Daddy spells it just D-U, and so do I because I am a junior. Why is that?"

Mother smiled gently.

"Daddy changed the way he spelled it," she said.

"Yes, I can see that," I persisted. "But *why* did he?"

"Well, Watty. It was before I met him. A long time before, in all those bachelor years of his, when he used to go out to the fashionable houses of his friends on Long Island and in New Jersey. They were very elegant, and he thought Doumaux looked a little like a peasant name. So he dropped the O to make it look a bit more elegant."

Her lips pressed together firmly—an indication that discussion was closed. But I persisted.

"*I* don't see why," I said, perhaps too loudly. "Was Daddy ashamed of Grandmother?"

93

"Of course not," Mother replied in a voice colder than I had ever heard her use, and I knew enough to drop the subject for good and all.

However, when I was back in my room once more, I brought out Father's signature and as I studied it I thought I understood why the *D* looked as if he had made it in anger. I also felt that Mother did not approve of his changing the spelling, though she regarded his doing to indulgently. As I studied the *D, I* also began to feel angry. Not at the name, but at his being angry about it. Instinctively I took up my pencil and without tracing paper made a capital *D* that seemed to me exactly like Father's.

I had no more time for forgery that afternoon, but the next day I began signing *Walter D. Edmonds* in full. The first few times I used tracing paper, but I began to feel so confident that I shifted to freehand writing. I was sure that I was turning out respectable forged signatures. Elation swept over me. In the flush of it, I did another and I thought that it was very nearly perfect.

By then it had come supper time, but I was happy to end my work on such a high note.

There were still details to master, for a check was more than just a signature. I would have liked to have one from Father's checkbook, but that was not possible. After worrying over the problem for several days, I finally hit on a solution. For the next few afternoons I cased the library, to use current vernacular. Then on a day when Alice was having time off, I slipped in with my tracing paper and ruler and made two facsimiles of one of Father's checks. Naturally they were simplified versions. I did not trouble to reproduce the check numbers or the codes. But the lines and spacing were exactly the same. With these, from which I could make other tracings, I returned to headquarters and practiced writing checks. Every one to me from my father. Doing my name was not difficult. It was without the loops and flourishes, as if my middle name was spelled D-o-u-maux.

Not till the first Sunday in April, having by then written and signed heaven only knows how many checks to myself, did I consider making my great attempt. As it turned out, luck played into my hands. I had developed a slight cold, so Mother decreed that I should not accompany her to church. Father, as usual, had started to pay the monthly bills; but when Mother came into him to report my cold and the fact that brother John had gone off to lunch at a friend's house uptown, he decided that she should not go unescorted and got up from his desk. Ten minutes later I had the library to myself.

The library was entirely Father's room. When 18 West Eleventh Street was built, no thought had been given for providing a den for the senior male, so my father had taken possession of the library as his natural right. His stamp was everywhere. Over the high mantelpiece of the black marble fireplace was a caribou head. He had regarded it, immediately after shooting the animal, as the most graceful he had ever seen; and it *was* beautiful, with a cool serenity persisting even on that high wall. (All three of the ground floor rooms had fourteen-foot ceilings.)

On the opposite wall was another caribou with antlers far heavier and with a wider spread—what sportsmen referred to as a "museum trophy." Unlike its vis-à-vis, this caribou bull had very obviously been lord of his domain. A sultry menace still emanated from that portentous head. On each side and just below each of these specimens were the front feet, mounted on oblongs of highly polished oak, the hoof fixed to the wood, and about ten inches of the leg bent upright to parallel the wall, the top ending in a silver cap. Even then I considered these feet so placed to be ridiculous—like spraying perfume on a rose. But the combination of those lofty gazes high above the head of an eleven-year-old boy, seated at a desk where he had no business at all to be, was distinctly daunting.

At my back, too, was one of Father's great Canadian trout, mounted behind a bell of molded glass. This was on one side of the caribou head. On the other was a group of photographs of Father in Canada or of his guides displaying strings of a day's catch of trout, now and then with captions in his writing, such as "smallest 3½ pounds, largest 7."

Against the inside wall stood an old French secretary that Father had spotted in an auction hall on one of his daily walks uptown from his Nassau Street office and bid successfully for. He said it had five secret drawers, but he had shown me only two of them, so it contained some of the mysteries that I associated with his person. The outer wall had three windows that reached nearly from floor to ceiling, through which all winter long on clear days sunshine poured in because the building opposite was only one story high.

When he first viewed the house, my father had observed this and before closing with the house agent had walked around to Tenth Street, introduced himself to the owner, Mr. Auerbach, and with great politeness inquired whether there was any possibility of stories being added in the future. No, said Mr. Auerbach, the one story building housed his personal library and he had no intention of increasing it to the dimensions of a second story. Father returned and bought our house then and there.

That Sunday morning on which I reached the crisis of my winter's striving, was clear and the library was flooded with sunlight, so comfortable and warm that for a moment I thought the two great caribou were dozing. But as soon as I seated myself in Father's chair, I felt that their eyes were on me. Even though he was several blocks away with Mother in Grace Church, his presence seemed to close around my small and insignificant body. It took an enormous effort of will to take his penholder from its tray and look down at the open check book.

Father had made his decision to accompany Mother to church at the point of finishing a check. It lay, still affixed to the stub, under my eyes. It was made out to one Alfred Balboa (to this day I have not the faintest idea of who Mr. Balboa was or what service he had furnished) for seventy-five dollars. I dipped the pen in ink and drew a deep breath to steady myself.

For the past three weeks, I had been making signatures with a Falcon nib abstracted from the little box of nibs in his desk drawer. It had presented difficulties and I had been disheartened until I chanced to see him change to a new nib and was later able to recover the used one from the waste basket. Use had made it conform to his peculiar hand and with it my confidence was restored.

I tried the pen from the tray on a sheet of the pad I had had the foresight to bring with me. It felt quite comfortable and the signature I wrote with it looked reassuringly like the one on the check before me. I took in another deep breath, blowing out my cheeks with it before I permitted myself to exhale. Then without a hesitation, I drew a check to Walter D. Edmonds, Jr. for a thousand dollars. I made the entry in the stub. To my eyes it appeared routine and convincing.

I stared a moment at what I had done, almost in disbelief. Then I picked up my pad, slipped out of the library, and stole away upstairs, passing the reproduction of Venus de Milo in her nitch at the curve to the second floor landing, grateful that she offered no comment.

———

Perhaps time is the most critical element in any enterprise, whether it be legal or illegal. As I sat in the window of my third floor room, looking down on Eleventh Street, I thought back on the hours, afternoons, occasionally even days that it had taken to prepare for those minutes in the library. But now the minutes spent waiting for my father and mother to return from church seemed inordinately longer. I hardly thought my life would be long enough. A numbness crept into my arms and legs. When at last I saw their foreshortened figures on the sidewalk turning into our brownstone front steps, it was as much as I could do to get out of my chair and creep to the bannister railing that fenced off the third floor landing from the stairwell.

Looking over the railing as inconspicuously as possible, I watched them in the hall below. Their voices came up clearly. "A lovely service," Mother said. "I hope Watty's cold has not got worse."

As a matter of fact my cold, whether from overreaction of adrenal glands or whatever reason, had evaporated.

"I don't see why it should have got worse," Father said, checking his appearance in the front hall mirror as was his wont before removing his hat and gloves. "You pamper your children far too much, Sally."

"I think," Mother said, "I'll just go up and have a moment's rest before dinner."

"Yes, do," said Father. "I'll be in the library. I still have some bills to pay."

Mother came up the stairs, her skirts rustling with a faint whisper such as some wings make in flight. Usually it brought feelings to my heart unrecognizable to me and mingled my emotions so that I felt both pain and pleasure. But now my entire attention was directed to my father's upright figure disappearing through the wide doors into the parlor. From the parlor he would pass through the dining room and then into the library. I knew to a tick or two of my Christmas watch exactly how long that would be. But I heard nothing.

Silence persisted and persisted, absolute and chilling. Then he appeared at the foot of the first flight of stairs.

"Sally," he called in a voice so low that it took me completely by surprise. "Sally. I must talk to you."

He was carrying the checkbook open in his hands.

Mother, whose hearing was sharper than a deer's, appeared directly under me, as she leaned over the rail of the second floor landing.

"What is it, Gridgey?" she asked quietly.

"I want you to look at this," he said, coming up the stairs, the checkbook extended before him. "I cannot understand what I have done. Just look at this."

Taking the checkbook from Father she studied it and then observed, "You've drawn a check to Watty for a thousand dollars. Why?"

"I don't know why! I don't know what I did. I drew that check to Alfred Balboa just before leaving to go with you to church. Usually I tear the check out as soon as I've signed it. I didn't this time. It's still there, as you see. But that check to Watty was under it when we came home."

Mother's voice contained a shadow of a smile.

"Then, Gridgey, someone else must have written that check while we were at church. Who do you suppose it could have been?"

My father's head reared back. In his ringing courtroom voice he called, "Watty!"

I had drawn back, but now I put my head where it could be seen and met the bleak blue stare of Father's eyes.

"Do you know anything about this check I've drawn to you for a thousand dollars?"

"You didn't write it," I said, swallowing my heart back down. "I did."

"*You* did?" shouted Father. "How do you mean, you did?"

"I said it would be easier to copy a signature like yours with those loops in it," I reminded him. "I wanted to show you it was."

"By God!" my father said. "I wouldn't have believed it. Didn't I tell you forgery was a crime?"

"Yes, but I didn't cash the check. I didn't want to cash it. I just wanted to forge your signature."

My mother, too, was looking up at me. The smile I had heard in her voice had been transferred to her lips. She turned back to Father.

"He's right, I think, Gridgey. He won't do it again. You won't will you, Watty?"

"No," I promised, with my whole soul behind the word. My relief was indescribable. There had been moments when I had envisioned jail. Apparently I had proved myself right and Father wrong and got away with it. All was coming right in my small world.

Mother had gone back into her own room and Father had reached the bottom of the stairs when suddenly he wheeled and shouted up at the top of his voice, "Sally! Sally! Sally!"

Mother reappeared below me but Father gave her no chance to speak.

"Sally! Let me tell you. And mark my words! That boy was born to be hanged!"

Bar a month or two he said that seventy years ago.

Josephine feeding tidbits to a few of the huge flock of turkeys. (150 were raised each summer; young broiled turkeys were delicious. We had turkey eggs for many breakfasts.) Josephine was the only female assistant Oscar of the Waldorf ever accepted. Everything from her kitchen was ambrosial. She finally fell a hopeless prey to gin and Mother wept when she dismissed her.

Irish Stew

A s nearly as I can remember, the weather that summer of 1914 was exceptionally beautiful. Haying proceeded with scarcely a hitch. Cloudless day followed cloudless day while the great loads creaked over the meadows until the whole barn was filled with the scent of new and perfectly cured hay. The idea that Europe might be teetering on the brink of a great and terrible war was inconceivable. Of course an eleven-year-old boy like myself never thought of it at all. But I was concerned about the domestic peace of Mother's household which, it seemed to me, might be about to end.

In my passage through the kitchen and maids' dining room on my way to the back stairs I had been hearing a word or two now and then, darkly uttered, that wakened an uneasiness in my mind. I knew that the cool tranquility of Northlands depended entirely on Mother's ability to keep the servants reasonably contented. That was not easy. Our nearest neighbor in any direction was more than a mile away. We did not have a telephone. Electricity, for our farm, was twenty years in the future. No one had a radio. Television was not even dreamed of. Because people in the two farm households across the brook looked askance on any-one who seemed "foreign," the maids had only each other to talk to and a grievance for one was almost certain to become the common cause.

This summer's grievance had begun with Tilly, not yet eighteen, the laundress who doubled as chambermaid. Tilly was the only one of the three who had been at Northlands before and the reason she wanted to come back was because in the preceding summer she had formed an attachment, as the saying was in those days, for one of the farm hands, a young fellow named Harlan Twichel. But to her dismay, within an hour of our arrival from the city, she learned that Harlan had left the farm. To make it worse for her he had left in order to get married to a girl who, three months after the wedding, had produced a baby Twichel. Even so, Tilly's heartache might have been assuaged had Harlan's replace-ment been a young and personable man. But Lincoln John, who managed the farm for Father, was fed up with young and unreliable young men and had hired instead a small and rather wizened Welshman in his late sixties. At her first glimpse of Heman Evans, Tilly knew herself to be bereft.

To do her justice she did not make a big production of her grief, but she went about her work with looks so woe-begone that my eleven-year-old heart was wrung; once or twice I heard her quietly weeping behind her closed bed-room door as I passed on my way to the back stairs, and became aware for the first time of how bitter for some people life could be. But while Tilly muffled her sorrow with modest diffidence, the other maids, especially Hannah the cook, became outspoken about what they called the shabby treatment the poor girl had received.

"As if I were to blame," Mother exclaimed resentfully. "I didn't know Harlan had left and wouldn't have cared if I had known. I had no idea how much Tilly cared for the wretched young man."

Ordinarily when trouble began to brew among her domestic staff Mother relied on Father for moral support. He could exert authority in a way that to a small boy of uncertain rectitude was positively awesome. But by now he had returned to New York City, where one of his cases was coming up for trial, and Mother had only her own resources to draw on. "If only I can manage to keep them from leaving until Daddy comes back," she said, more to herself than to me. And now, though Tilly's unhappiness continued to sadden me, I became equally disturbed by Mother's apprehensions. I tried to think of something I could say or do to make the maids feel happier, but I knew there was nothing. Even at that early stage of my existence I had learned that resentment, once it became established among the help, was a malady that grew in unpredictable ways and was unstoppable, for it seemed to feed upon itself. It made me think of the Hydra in my book of Greek myths, which grew two heads to replace any one of its nine you might succeed in cutting off. Hercules finally destroyed it, but here at Northlands there was only my mother to confront the hydra of the maids discontent and, brave and beautiful though she was in my eyes, she was no Hercules.

Every morning, half an hour after breakfast, I could sense her inner mustering of resolution as she left the living room for the kitchen to plan with Hannah the day's meals. She returned from these sessions troubled and distracted. But one morning she reentered the living room with cheeks flushed and flaming eyes and when I asked what the matter was, for this was an aspect of my mother I had never seen, she answered with an uncharacteristic bite in her voice, "Those girls are impossible. Nothing I say makes the least difference to them. I *told* them last spring that we lived way off from anybody else. But *they* say I never told them how *lonely* it was. And they say I don't order nice meals for them, as if our milk and eggs and meat from the farm and the fresh garden vegetables were't better than anything they could ever get in city markets."

She drew a deep breath, and I saw that she was trembling. "They are outrageous! They will be giving notice next. I wish," she went on, making each word emphatic, "we still had public whipping posts, the way they used to have down South!"

I stared at her, astonished and distrubed. She sounded utterly unlike the gentle person I had always known as Mother. Into my mind, unbidden, out of nowhere, burst an image of Tilly at the whipping post. Why Tilly, I do not know; perhaps because she was the nearest of the maids to my own age. Illustrations in the antislavery books behind the glass fronts of the parlor book cases, books that had come down from my Abolitionist great-grandfather, gave form to my imagination. I saw Tilly's joined hands tied to the whipping post above her head, stretching her so that she stood on tiptoe, her thin back shrinking in expectation of the lash. I was guiltily aware that a boy like me was not supposed to have such thoughts, but that did nothing to diminish the vividness of what in my mind's eye I saw.

My mother was looking at me.

"Of course," she said, "I did not really mean that, Watty. It's just that I'm at my wits' end."

Her smile was oddly hesitant, even apologetic. I nodded, having no notion of what I should say; and in a moment, I left the room, beset with apprehensions of I did not know exactly what. Perhaps for the first time I had become uncertain of the essential rightness of everything my mother said and stood for. I went upstairs and down the long hall that led to the children's bedrooms at the rear of the house. As I reached the end I heard footsteps laboriously climbing the back stairs. The door banged open and Tilly blundered through lugging a laundry basket loaded with sheets and towels still fragrant from her ironing. To my eyes it seemed a load too heavy for somebody so slight, but as we passed each other—I to my room and she to the linen closet to sort and put away her wash—she turned her head to me and smiled.

It was the first time I had seen her smile since she had learned of Harlan Twichel's departure. I didn't know what to make of it. For a while I stood at my window, gazing at the brook as it poured down the rust brown slide of granite, and trying to understand what had made Tilly smile; but when, after ten or fifteen minutes, the sheep bells rang for lunch in the downstairs hall, I was just as puzzled as before. To make things even stranger Kathleen, the waitress, came through the pantry door with a bright smile of her own.

She had a message for Mother. "Mr. John," she said, "was just in the kitchen, Mam, and asked to tell you he'll be cutting up the lamb after you've had your lunch, if you'd wish to come over."

Mother either did not notice Kathleen's smile or, if she did, thought nothing of it. So she, like me, was taken aback

107

when Kathleen appeared at the carriage barn with a note from Hannah giving notice on behalf of all three maids.

———————

One of the things I most enjoyed in the routine of the farm was to watch my mother and Lincoln John in consultation over the butchering of a lamb, calf, or pig. The carcass, skinned and dressed and wiped clean, hung from its iron gambrel in the wide, open doorway. Even on the hottest day there always seemed to be a stir of air through the door, perhaps from the breeze the brook generated in its rush down the granite slide to the rapids below the buildings. The carcass had become strangely impersonal, to which Mother and Lincoln John in my eyes made an electrifying contrast. She looked immaculately cool in a wide brimmed Leghorn hat, white shirtwaist striped with lavender, piqué stock, and soft tan skirt, graceful and slender waisted; I thought no other being beautiful as she breathed on earth. Lincoln John, more than a head taller in spite of his stooped shoulders, massive, with the slow movements of a man who takes great strength for granted, had on a clean white shirt for the occasion, as he invariably did, the sleeves hitched up from his wrists with black arm garters, and a hard straw boater hat of the sort professional butchers wore. He raised his meat saw as though in salute and with remarkable swiftness sawed down the length of the backbone from crotch to throat. Then, one in each hand, he lifted the two halves down from the gambrel and laid them side by side on his cutting table. Together he and Mother looked down in shared pleasure at a piece of work professionally done; then without speaking Mother reached out and drew an imaginary line over the white carcass with a white-gloved fingertip. Lincoln John ducked his head in something like a bow and the butcher knife, which in his great hand looked utterly inconsequential, made the first cut in exact conformance to her indicated line. He glanced sidelong towards her for approval; she gave a smiling nod; and he smiled in return: all done with the sedate and elegant formality of two people dancing a pavane in a medieval court.

The winter after Lincoln John first came to manage the farm Mother had gone to the butcher she patronized in Jefferson Market for lessons in the art of meat cutting and the following summer had begun these sessions of teacher and pupil. By now, many years later, Lincoln John knew just as well as she how to cut up a carcass of lamb, veal, or pork, as well as the proper way to dress chickens, ducks, and turkeys. She knew that, and he knew that she knew; but neither of them would have dreamed of giving up their ceremonial exchange. I was aware of that, too, and sat on my upturned bucket against the wall, watching the byplay between them with the absorption and curiosity a child feels in the mysteries of adult behavior. To all three, of us therefore, I think, Kathleen's arrival was, in one way or another, a shock.

Mother took Hannah's missive, penciled on a small sheet of ruled note paper, from the tray Kathleen held out, glanced at it, and said, "Thank you, Kathleen. You may tell Hannah I shall speak to her when I get back to the house."

109

Kathleen made a small bob and looked embarrassed.

"Excuse me, Mam, but Hannah said I was to bring her the organs."

Mother, whose cheeks had flushed, seemed momentarily distracted, but Lincoln John reached for a yellow earthenware bowl, in which he had set aside the liver, kidneys, and sweetbreads, and without comment placed it on Kathleen's tray. Then he and Mother resumed cutting up the lamb as if nothing whatever had occurred.

It was not until we were crossing the bridge on our way back to the house that she said, "They have given notice, all three, as I expected." She broke off, and I saw she was biting her lip. It was plain to me that she was troubled in her thoughts. But she said nothing until we were mounting the porch steps to the front door. "Those miserable girls!" she exclaimed. "I don't know how I can tell Daddy. He's going to be dreadfully upset."

I wanted to go to the kitchen with her when she went to see Hannah, but she said "No"; so I waited in the living room. She came back after only a few minutes. Her color was still high, but she seemed a good deal less agitated. "At least," she told me, "they are honoring their two weeks' notice," and with obvious relief added, "Daddy should be back before then."

She expected him at the end of the week, on the Saturday afternoon train, but as matters turned out he came back on Friday. Mother went to meet him at the depot, driven by Lincoln John in the covered surrey. Lincoln John sometimes said that when my father came back from the city "it tightened up the whole place." This did not seem to me exactly true because as I listened to his and Father's discussions about what needed doing and how it should be done, it always turned out in the end to be done according to Lincoln John's own plans. But I knew what Lincoln John meant: Father's manner was decisive. Now, as he got out of the carriage and helped Mother down, I could see that a good deal of her apprehension had been allayed. Father would take charge. He believed, to use a phrase frequently employed by one of Mother's distinguished nautical relations, in running a tight ship.

I had therefore expected that he would have Hannah come to the living room right away. To talk to her in the kitchen, which she naturally considered her own territory, was not his style; he believed in "calling them on the carpet" as he put it, sitting in his arm chair while they stood in front of him. I think Mother had also expected an immediate confrontation, even counted on it. But Father refused to alter the usual procedures he observed whenever he returned to Northlands, which over the years had gained an almost ritual significance. His first action was to draw himself a glass of our icy cold spring water from the pantry faucet, declaring as he sipped it that it was the "purest water in all God's creation." Then he went upstairs "to get into his Northlands clothes."

Clothes were important to my father. He was at ease only when he considered himself to be appropriately dressed. Long after most lawyers had given up such formal garb he went off to his downtown office wearing a cutaway and striped dress trousers, usually with a snow white dickey to edge the neckline of his waistcoat. The daily process of selection of which coat, which trousers, which waistcoat and which necktie, had fascinated me since early childhood. It was serious business and sometimes invested with considerable drama. And now, when he came down to the living room for tea, he was as carefully dressed as on any morning in the city, though in his conception of what a gentleman should wear on his country estate.

Knickerbockers with thin, tan felt knee-cuffs were de rigueur. A jacket of natural linen (replaced in fall by one of Canadian homespun), brogues of white elkskin which were specially ordered from Abercrombie and Fitch, and instead of the usual detachable collar, a madras stock that served as both collar and tie, surrounding his throat with a band of bright colors and tying in front in a neat, narrow bow. I had never seen anyone else wear one (nor have I since). I admired his appearance exceedingly.

At this time he had abandoned the dark beard that characterized my earliest recollection of him in favor of a mustache, which he wore with its points turned dramatically up in the style of the Emperor of Germany. To ensure its maintaining this militant form throughout the day he put on each night what, in the barbering trade, was known as a kaiserbund, a device of gauze and celluloid with elastic loops to go over the ears, which held the dampened mustache in the proper shape until it dried. No doubt, I thought in small-boy fashion, the Kaiser used one, too, in order to keep his mustache as perfect as my father's. I had seen pictures of the German emperor; not even with his uniforms and medals did he seem more formidable than Father—especially now as he waited in his big chair for Hannah to appear.

"Go with Mother, Watty," he said, after we had had tea. "I want to see Hannah alone."

I had lingered as unobtrusively as possible when Mother left the room, hoping to witness Hannah's confrontation, but the tone of his voice left no choice. I went, passing Hannah in the hall. To my surprise she exhibited no sign of alarm or even apprehension. Her long face was as dourly set as desert stone. She closed the door behind her and I heard Father's muffled voice but not what he said. I could hear nothing from Hannah at all and presently I retreated to the parlor so as not to be caught eavesdropping.

In a few minutes Hannah came out of the living room and returned to her kitchen without the least discernible change in her expression. My mother appeared from where I had no idea and together we went back to Father. The high color of his cheeks had noticeably darkened. He looked for the moment nonplussed, and angry.

"That woman," he said, "is impervious to reason. She has the heart of a vulture. She is incorrigible!"

"Oh, Gridgey," cried Mother, "what are we going to do? If just Hannah were to go, or even two of them, we might manage. That is, as long as Kathleen was the one who stayed."

"Hannah says they are all going to leave," Father said grimly. His ice blue stare turned on me, and for a moment my mind cast about like a panic-stricken rabbit's for something I had done to which the maids' departure might be attributed. But Father's eye passed on and I drew a careful breath.

"I shall think about it overnight," he said, "and decide tomorrow what we ought to do. But I'll be damned, Sally," he added in his ringing courtroom voice, "if I'll let three heedless, ignorant maids spoil the rest of our summer."

The staring blue gaze swung around to me and for an uncomfortable moment I again ran over my activities, this time for the past several days, for any possible malfeasances. Somewhat to my surprise I could think of none, and venturing to raise my eyes I found his gaze still fixed upon me. Intuitively I knew that he had already reached a decision.

"Watty," he said, "I'll be driving over to Forestport tomorrow morning. There's someone I want to see there and I'll need somebody to hold the horse while I'm in his house. Will you come with me?"

Though I knew it was a command, not a question, I said I would be glad to, and meant it.

———————

We drove into the village about an hour before noon. The narrow dirt road became River Street but, except that there were houses close together it was still a dirt road along which we drove barely a hundred yards before my father turned the buggy and pulled up in front of the Catholic church.

"Hold onto these," he said, handing me the reins. "Don't let them out of your hands. I shan't be long."

He paused to look up at the front of the church: its neatly painted white clapboard walls and the brown shingled cupola-like structure above the gable that served both as belfry and steeple; then turned immediately towards the rectory next door, a small, shabby building, desperately in need of paint. He went up the front steps, compact, rigidly erect, exuding, I thought, unlimited authority.

He turned the bell handle in the middle of the front door and the ringing, rather like that of a bicycle, only

114

coarser and seven times as loud, sounded all the way out to the street, even alerting two hens in the barnyard opposite who came over with fidgety footsteps to prospect between the buggy wheels for possible good fortune from above. By the time I looked back to the rectory, my father had disappeared inside.

Waiting was tedious. For a while I watched the hens. Then I tried counting the flies on Dick's hind quarters. It grew hotter as the sun came over the tops of the maples. I wondered what my father was talking about to the priest. To my surprise the priest's name came into my mind—Father Dinsmore it was—and I decided I must have heard it from Lincoln John.

Usually, during the few times my father and I found ourselves together, he had little to say to me. Once or twice, however, he did speak about his practice and the law: how best to present the particular brief on which he was then engaged to the judge who had been scheduled to hear the case, enumerating the judge's idiosyncracies and known prejudices, casting himself as David going forth against the Goliath of the Law—and though I was aware that comment from me was neither expected nor desired, my sympathy for him became almost unbearably keen. And now, visualizing him beyond the blank front door of the rectory, face to face with Father Dinsmore, whom I imagined, for whatever reason, to be a big and formidable man, I fell prey to new anxieties.

When, therefore, the front door finally opened and my father emerged onto the stoop with the priest behind him, I was taken by surprise, for Father Dinsmore was a small, unassuming man in a shabby soutane, with a thin, pale, and rather sad face. It lit up briefly as Father turned to shake hands; they shared for a moment a mutual and satisfactory understanding. They looked to me very much like two men who had arrived at agreement over a horse.

Father was still looking pleased when he got into the buggy and took the reins from my hands, but he also seemed thoughtful. Instead of starting Dick up with a touch of the buggy whip, as was his custom, in order to establish his authority, he merely shook the reins and clicked his tongue, as Lincoln John would have done or, as I told myself, I myself would have. Dick, like the honoest horse he was, in three strides had broken into his swift and surging trot, and Father for once seemed content to let him choose his own pace.

But I was curious about what Father and the priest had been discussing behind that closed front door. It seemed important that I should know. I listened to the squeak of the buggy wheels on the dry dirt road. Dick turned the corner at Corcoran's little fish hatchery pond and started up the first of the two hills that would bring us up on the sand flats and Kruscome's meager farm. The grade slowed him to a walk.

"If Father Dinsmore a nice man?" I asked finally, not being able to think of a better way of getting us back to the rectory.

"What do you mean 'a nice man'?" demanded Father. "Why shouldn't he be nice?"

"I don't know," I said. "I just wondered."

"Well," Father said, "we got along well enough. We understood each other. You might almost say," and he allowed himself a small smile, "that we saw eye to eye."

We were passing between the house and barn, both small and shabby buildings, where the Szlabowski family, recently arrived from Poland, eked out a living with six cows and some chickens, and Dick again slowed to a walk for the pull up the second hill. The upper third was all soft sand, which made the going hard; but once on top of the sand flats the road surface hardened and Dick once more broke into his driving trot.

It was always exhilarating to ride behind Dick when he was pouring on the pace, and we came down off the sand flats full tilt, past Daubach's wood lot, and then onto our own property. Ahead, suddenly, there was a large fat woodchuck scurrying down the right hand rut. Father spotted him and reached for the whip, but Dick needed no urging, for he had seen the woodchuck, too, and his competitive instinct had become red hot. In an instant we were really flying. Our wheels were almost on him when at the last split second the woodchuck wrenched himself out of the rut, lost his balance on the shoulder of the road, and went spinning end over end down the bank. Dick hardly slackened his pace; his blood was up, and we tore past the foot of the pond and down the long grade to the river road (for Father would never drive, nor allow himself to be driven, home by the back entrance) and came up the front drive, still at a spanking trot, with Dick showing lather on his neck and shoulders that made Lincoln John shake his head in silent disapproval.

I had hoped to hear what Father might say to Mother, but he led her into the living room, closing the door behind them, and he must have kept his voice down, for I could not hear a word.

The rest of Saturday passed uneventfully. The kitchen atmosphere was cool, one might say poised, but revealed no hostile edges. Luncheon and dinner went smoothly enough. If Kathleen offered no smile, her waiting was quick and neat so that even Father could find nothing to complain of. Breakfasts on Sunday we served ourselves, for the maids were driven over to Forestport for early mass in the open buckboard if the day was sunny, or in the covered surrey if weather threatened.

Our oatmeal porridge waited for us on the black Glenwood stove (then considered upstate the ultramodern of kitchen ranges) in a double boiler from which a thread of steam still issued; corned beef hash was ready on its platter in the warming oven; it only remained to prepare my father's poached egg, which he expected no matter what other breakfast might be served; and this task my mother addressed, as she always did, with considerable agitation. Fortunately that morning all went well and we were leaving the table when the rattle of planks on the bridge over the brook announced the return of the maids.

A few minutes later Kathleen appeared at the living room door with a beaming smile. She even curtsied as she said, "Excuse me, Mam, but Hannah is asking might she be having a word with you and the Mister."

"Why yes," Mother replied. "She can come any time."

Kathleen smiled again as she left and Hannah appeared so promptly that she must have been waiting just outside the door. She wore no smile, but it seemed to me that her forbidding face had lost some of its animosity. She still looked formidable, standing squarely in front of my seated father and mother. She resembled, I thought, a stubborn horse, which made what she now said all the more amazing.

"Me and the girls have been talking things over and we would like to stay on till the end of the summer, if that will suit you, Mister and Missus."

For a moment my mother looked positively dazed. Then a tide of blessed relief flooded her face. But her voice when she spoke was cool and matter of fact.

"Are you sure about this, Hannah?"

"Yes, Mam," Hannah replied, equally cool and matter of fact.

"Well," Mother said. "I'm glad you girls have had this change of heart. Let's just go on as if it had been this way all along."

Hannah nodded and turned to withdraw. Kathleen, who with Tilly had appeared in the door, gave us her flashing smile. Tilly, in an evident state of bemusement, recollected herself and bobbed a curtsey before following the other two into the hall.

Mother drew in a long breath of relief as she watched them go. "How extraordinary! I can hardly believe it's true."

"Don't worry, dear," my father said. "We have to accept miracles now and then, whether we believe in them or not."

An expression of complacence sat rather oddly on his face, but disappeared as his eyes met mine. He stared hard at me as if he had an admonition of some sort in mind; but when in sudden uneasiness I looked down at my sneakers, he turned away without saying anything. I was able to escape from the house to the farm buildings where, it being Sunday, nothing to interest me was going on.

It seemed no time at all, however, before I heard the hand bell ringing on the kitchen porch, announcing that it was half an hour to dinner and that children such as I should come in to wash. I could tell that Kathleen was the ringer, for in her hand the bell notes sounded bright and gay. When Tilly swung the bell, the notes were nowhere near as loud and almost apologetic. In Hannah's hand, which happened rarely, the summons sounded like the crack of doom.

Before I reached the kitchen door, I smelled the roasting beef, a special treat during our Northlands summer. For though the farm supplied us with lamb and veal and pork, and chickens galore, Father never made arrangements to raise a steer. Hannah had the roast half out of the oven and was basting it. As each spoonful of dripping ran over the meat the mouth-watering aroma intensified.

"It smells wonderful," I said.

"It ought to. It's a fine roast," Hannah said, basting three or four spoonsful more before shoving the roast back and closing the oven door. My eye fell on a black iron pan on top of the stove, covered by a tin lid.

"What's that, Hannah?"

"Irish stew," she replied.

"What are you cooking that for now?" I asked. "Along with the beef?"

"It's for *our* dinner," Hannah answered shortly.

"But why? The roast looks plenty big enough to go around."

"The roast's too grand for the likes of us," she said.

I felt I ought to say something, but I couldn't think what; and Hannah went on with her work as if I didn't exist. It seemed better to leave her alone, so I went through the kitchen dining room and up the back stairs to my bedroom with a distinct feeling that something somehow was not all that it should be. The feeling was still with me when the sheep bells sounded in the front hall and I went down to the dining room.

The roast, when Kathleen carried it in and placed it in front of Father, was truly magnificent. Father picked up the carving knife and, after testing the edge delicately with the end of his index finger, reached for the steel. For a few seconds the chill whisper of the steel caressing the blade was the only sound in the room. Then Fater said, "It looks like an excellent roast, my dear."

"Mr. Neejer promised me that it would be good," she said, her voice striking a hopeful note, but at the same time she looked pleased, and my father addressed himself to his work. He remained seated while he carved, it being his contention that only someone inept and unskilled had to stand. The slices slid beautifully off the ribs as we watched. He was precise and delicate as he put the outside slice and the next on a plate for my mother, adding a roast potato and spooning some of the growing reservoir of dripping over all.

Kathleen picked up the plate, replacing it with another she had been holding in her other hand. I watched as she exchanged the plate with beef and potato with the empty one in front of Mother and returned with it to Father, still wearing her smile. I thought that she enjoyed what she was doing; the whole procedure seemed to me admirable in its efficiency and, as she performed it, grace. When she had put the final plate in front of me, she went out to the pantry to

121

fetch the vegetable, whatever it might be. I never knew what
it was because, all of a sudden, I heard myself say, "It's
wrong!" in a loud voice. It was something I'd had no intention of saying, though I suppose I must subconsciously have
had, for right away, without being able to stop myself, I said
again, "It's all wrong!" even louder. And then I became
aware of all the family, in their seats around the table, looking at me in astonishment. Yet not one of them was as
astonished as I was.

Mother was the first to find her voice. "What is it
that's wrong, Watty?" she asked.

I did not really know what was wrong, what I thought
was wrong. It nagged somewhere at the back of my mind.
But I could see the rapidly increasing disapproval, even
distaste, in my father's face. I had to find something to
account for my outburst. And then like a blessing for the
discovered sinner, the rich remembered smell of lamb as
Hannah lifted the lid off the pan of Irish stew came to me
and I said again, "It's all . . . " But Father interrupted tes-
tily, "For Heaven's sake, let's leave this till Kathleen has
passed the vegetable."

So we sat in silence while Kathleen went around the
table, this time without a smile, and disappeared into the
pantry. What the vegetable was I can't recall; I don't think
I even saw what I put on my plate.

"Now," said Father, "tell us what you think is wrong."

"I don't see why," I began, but now I could hardly get
my voice to function. A moment ago words had come out
of my mouth in almost a bellow; for some reason my voice
had faded until I could barely hear myself what I was saying. I tried to clear my throat as Father said, "Speak up,

can't you! That is, if you really have something to tell us."
His face had assumed one of its most forbidding aspects.
Across the table my older brother watched me with a skep-
tical grin. My little sister gazed at me open-mouthed. Only
my mother's face seemed sympathetic.

"I don't see why we should be having roast beef and
the maids have to eat Irish stew."

"What's wrong with Irish stew?" demanded Father.

"Nothing, I guess. Only it doesn't taste as good as
roast beef. It isn't fair."

I was still having difficulty with my voice. Father again
exhorted me not to mumble. "And stand up while you're
about it. A lawyer always stands to address the court. I take
it you intend to plead for the servants."

I tried to ignore the sarcasm in his voice. Nor did
I see how a lawyer's conduct in a court room had anything to do with me. I was also scared at what I had
embarked on. But suddenly I found myself sustained by a
sense, quite new in my relatively brief existence, of moral
indignation.

"Anyway," I said, "I don't see why the maids have to
eat different food from ours. Aren't they people? Just like
us?"

"Of course they are people, Watty," Mother said. "But
they aren't 'just like us.' If they were, they would not be
working for us as servants."

I could not see how to answer that, but as I stumbled
for words my mother went on, "If you think we do not treat
the girls fairly, Watty, I promise you you are wrong. They
are much better off here than they would be in a great many
other situations. They each have their own room, for one

thing. And we do give them good food. Their Irish stew is made from Northlands lamb."

She said this with great emphasis. Father nodded approvingly. I remained unconvinced.

"If it's so good, why aren't we having it too, instead of the roast beef?" I asked. "Mummy said it was for a treat."

"It's a treat for us," said Mother.

"Why can't they have a treat, too?"

Having lost all patience, Father broke in.

"Whether you mean it or not you are being impertinent to your mother," he said, measuring his words. I knew the tone of voice and knew, also, that I was on a ragged edge. The delicious smell of the freshly carved slice on my plate overwhelmed my better judgement. "It isn't fair," I reiterated. "I think it's mean."

"Oh Watty," Mother said unhappily. "Don't say that!"

But Father had had enough. "If you feel that way, if you think we—your mother and I—are mean-spirited, you shouldn't eat with us. Go and eat with the maids. Irish stew will be more to your taste, no doubt."

I stared at him, transfixed. It wasn't what I had meant to say at all, yet somewhere inside me I felt that it was true.

"Go along," my father commanded, and I knew he would brook no more delay. I turned and left, blundering as I went through the pantry door.

At the other end of the pantry, the door to the kitchen was swinging very slightly, so I suspected that Kathleen must have lingered to listen to everything we'd said. My spirits lifted as it occurred to me that the maids would appreciate what I'd been saying in their behalf, and I passed into the kitchen ready to assume a hero's role.

———————

The maids' dining room opened on my right. Their table was against the wall: Hannah sitting with her back to the kitchen had a view of the brook running down and away through the meadows; Kathleen, opposite her, watched me come into the room, her face without expression; Tilly's place was at the side, between them, so she faced the wall. Of the three she seemed to me the only sympathetic one. None of them said a word. I stood awkwardly, staring back at them. Finally Hannah nodded with her head towards the far corner. An occasional table stood there. A kitchen chair had been placed in front of it, and on the table were a napkin, knife, and fork, and a plate of Irish stew.

"Your lunch," was all Hannah had to say.

I moved to the table in a trance. I sat down; my back was to the maids. I faced the corner. I could not understand what was happening. I had expected to be welcomed. Instead I was put into a corner. I looked down at the plate and felt my gorge begin to rise. I knew that if I put a single forkful in my mouth I would be violently sick. Yet instinctively I knew that everything I had said in the front dining room was true. It left me bewildered. Without saying a word I got up and left, laboriously climbing the back stairs to my room, and lay down on my bed without bothering to remove my sneakers.

It was my first first experience of the unpredictability of human nature, and I was perplexed, disheartened, and not a little frightened.

Oddly enough, our summer from then on went smoothly and was pleasant. The maids seemed to have worked off their resentments and at times seemed even to enjoy the life at Northlands. My outburst also appeared to have been forgotten, by both my family and the maids, though the mere sight of Irish stew for ever after has raised in me the spectre of instant nausea. Mother basked in the domestic tranquillity which she cherished above almost every other factor in our family life. But after the fifth of August when the New York papers began to report Germany's invasion of Belgium, my father became restless. Half French, he was totally enlisted in the cause of France. Overnight his mustache lost its upturned imperial aspect. I never saw the Kaiserbund again.

By late August, with German armies across the Marne, he had become frantic, though never losing confidence in the ultimate invincibility of France, and by mid-September the twenty-four hour, occasionally forty-eight hour, delay in receiving the news became more than he could stand. Ordinarily we stretched our Northlands summer till the day after Election, but in 1914 Father brought us back to New York before October.

Everyone else seemed pleased at the early return; the maids were openly delighted to find themselves back in the city. I alone was resentful. The winter months in New York were for me time to be served until the first of May once more returned us to Northlands. The war in Europe meant nothing to me. The only paper I read was the Boonville Herald that came from upstate once a week. It arrived on Fridays and no one touched it until Father had looked at it on Sunday morning. After that I was at liberty to read it if I wanted.

It was my only link with Northlands and I plodded through every story; even the reports of local doings from surrounding towns and villages sent in by a variety of correspondents. So it was that in the third week in November my eye was caught by *Forestport News,* in which the lead item stated that, thanks to the generosity of an anonymous benefactor, the repairs and renovation of St. Patrick's Rectory had finally been completed.

———

In my mind's eye I waited again on River Street, watching, in company with the two inquisitive hens, the door of the rectory open and my father emerging with Father Dinsmore behind him, shaking hands, and I had a pretty clear idea of what they had been talking about. In a confused way I understood what my outburst at that Sunday dinner had actually been about. Yet all that remained with me then, and has remained with me ever since, was my dislike of Irish stew.

Father with a varying hare, or Canadian hare, or snowshoe rabbit, and his black cocker, Colonel.

The Borgia Connection

During the early days of our childhood in New York it was Father's invariable custom to walk from our house on Eleventh Street to his law office downtown, at first at 31 Nassau Street but later on in Maiden Lane. He had been doing this since 1876 when he first began the practice of generel law as a very junior person in the offices of an established firm. But he soon turned his attention to the law of patents, quickly becoming a leading figure in the field, and opened an office of his own. Naturally, as a small boy I was unaware of such things, but the drama of my father's morning departure never failed to impress me.

It began half an hour before breakfast with the selection of what he was to wear: which of the striped dress trousers, of which there must have been ten or a dozen pairs; which of an almost equal number of cutaway coats and whether a waistcoat matching the cutaway or one of contrasting color and texture; which of the half dozen stacks of shirts or of the thirty-odd pairs of shoes; what necktie, out of dozens. This process was to a large extent affected by whether an appearance in court had been scheduled, which

129

of his clients he expected to meet. Weather and temperature had also to be considered and, since I was allowed to be on hand during all this decision-making, I was expected to read the thermometer outside the bedroom window just as, a little later, it was my duty to read aloud the condensed weather report in the upper right hand corner of the front page of the *Tribune*. When, very occasionally, he asked my opinion on a difficult choice and then agree, my day was made.

It was the moment of his departure, however, that was for me truly electrifying. He would come down the long flight from the second story and a final visit to the bathroom, from which he could be heard singing bits of opera, most often *Il Trovatore,* which signalized success, stop a moment by the hall table with a black marble top and the silver bowl for visiting cards, then reach to the coat rack for the appropriate overcoat. In winter this would be one of the coaching coats that had been tailor-made for him in England, gray tweed or, more often, tan whipcord, nearly ankle length and with a cape that reached below his shoulder blades and swung a little to the vigor of his stride. Then his hat. It might be a derby, but more likely a fedora. Father was one of the first men in New York City to wear one and his favorite was a light gray, like those the Prince of Wales wore in photographs in the *London Illustrated News*. Father was thought, especially by my mother's family, to look remarkably like the future King of England, an impression Mother herself, who had once been bumped into and knocked to the pavement by Edward, corroborated. And I think Father himself was not averse to enhancing this resemblance.

Now he had only to pull on his gloves and choose his cane before he stepped forth onto the brownstone stoop, tapped his hat to the proper angle, and went down to the pavement. From one of the parlor windows, my nose leaving an impression on the glass, I watched him set off for Fifth Avenue, until he turned the corner, striding south. He seemed to me a gallant figure. So Lancelot might issue forth on a mission of knight-errantry or Galahad leave Camelot in quest of the Grail.

I think now, looking back over so many years, that Father was not unaware of the effect he had on me. In fact, I should not be surprised if he did not share a bit of my admiration and even possibly enacted in his imagination some knightly role as he wove his vigorous way through the crowded sidewalk traffic that varied from block to block on his walk downtown. My reason for believing this stems from his recollections of the blizzard of 1888. Invariably the first snowfall of the season would fire his memory and all through breakfast he would tell my brother and me, and of course Mother, and for that matter the waitress if she wanted to listen from her post in the pantry, about how the snow began to fall on Sunday afternoon—it was the eleventh of March—how it snowed right through the night, and all the next day, and the next. He watched it from time to time from the windows of his apartment on Union Square, the same apartment to which he brought my mother after their wedding twelve years later. And it snowed through most of the third day, Wednesday. The city lay under a white suffocation: nothing moved, no delivery wagons, no cabs, no buses, no trolleys, all of which of course were horse-drawn—which meant that not even the Fire Department could respond to an alarm. For all their steam-powered engines even the elevated railways were unable to move. There was no way passengers could have got to them, in any case. Families ran out of milk, of provisions, of coal. What shocked my father most was, when he opened a window, the utter stillness. Four hundred people had died, but it was days before that became known.

On Thursday morning Father decided that somehow or other he would get downtown to his office. Sound had returned to the city. Not much sound: snow shovels, as caretakers and janitors began the Herculean task of opening paths along the sidewalks; the scrape of their shovels was muted by the depth of the snow they attacked.

Leaving an envelope containing some money and a note to his housekeeper in case she managed to get to her job, he set forth for Nassau Street. It took him four hours to walk the two miles. Where a householder had not yet cleared a path he had to break his way through snow sometimes more than waist deep. As he got farther down town and the buildings rose higher, the funneling wind had built drifts higher than the second-story windows. Often, in fact for the greater part of his remaining way, janitors and their helpers, unable to clear the sidewalks, had dug tunnels along the building walls. How they got rid of the snow thus dug was something Father never discovered. He would tell us how they eyed him as he pushed on, as though they were looking at somebody insane. "And I suppose," he liked to say, "by then I might have been a little bit so," adding, "in my absolute determination to reach my goal."

When at last he found himself at 31 Nassau Street, coming to the front entrance beneath Lord only knew how many feet of snow, members of the building's maintenance crew, at least those who had living quarters there, greeted him with open-mouthed astonishment—much, my father thought, as Robinson Crusoe must have greeted Friday. Even in the retelling after more than twenty years it was evident that he equated his performance with the exploits of heroes in mythology. And in my youthful state of eight or nine I, too, was convinced of his heroic stature.

My admiration knew no bounds. Every time he walked away through falling snowflakes I secretly wished that there might be another blizzard so that we might see him breasting his way back through drifts to our brownstone steps. But of course there never was another blizzard to compare with that of 1888. And Father, who had been fifty when he married, for the first time, in 1900, was already in his sixties, so that if there were more than two or three inches of snow he would forego the walk to his office and instead take the Sixth Avenue Elevated, which he boarded at Eighth Street, an action he rationalized by citing the responsibilities he now, as a married man, owed to his wife and little children. We, he was wont to say, had become his hostages to fortune. In summertime at the farm upstate he saw himself as Horatius, protecting his family and the white pillars of his home. Eighteen West Eleventh Street was more like a castle from which he issued every morning, a knight in armor to do battle with the world.

———————

It may sound simple, but getting my father into his "armor" was anything but that. In a minute written shortly after Father's death, Justice Augustus Noble Hand (brother of the more celebrated Learned Hand, though, in my father's estimation, a man infinitely more learned in the law) wrote: "His precision and exactitude in details and his careful attention to dress were things quite noticeable and not very common among our countrymen." Judge Hand ascribed this absorption in details to my father's being half-French. Others might have laid it to a natural vanity or, let us say, a natural self-appreciation. In any case, Father's daily preparations, lengthy and not always unstressful, had their fascinating aspects and, oddly enough, from the age of seven I began to take part in them.

This came about in a wholly fortuitous way. While my mother, my brother, and I waited in the library one morning for my father to come down to breakfast—though a stickler for punctuality in others he was apt to be late himself—Mother remembered a name and telephone number he had asked her to write down for him the night before. She wrote it out now and asked me to take it upstairs to him at once. It was a long flight in our old Federal house with its fourteen-foot ceilings so, in my hurry, I was panting as I passed the niche at the top where the treads curved to meet the landing under the benign but vacuous regard of the three-foot replica of the Venus de Milo. Sustained by my sense of importance, I ran along the landing to Father's bedroom door, knocked, and went in.

He looked startled, accepted Mother's note almost absently, and returned to his contemplation of three neckties laid out on the bed. One was a solid dark red, one was Navy blue, and the third black with a narrow red stripe.

"I can't make up my mind which is right for today," he said. "What do you think, Watty?"

I glanced at the clothes he had laid out. He was wearing what I thought were his best dress trousers. On the bed was the darkest of his cutaway coats, the waistcoat with it and, buttoned inside the edge of the opening, a white dickey. I knew Father wore a dickey only if he was meeting a major client or arguing a case in court. The dark gray cutaway seemed to indicate the latter.

"I wouldn't wear any of them," I said. I saw him stiffen.

"You wouldn't, would you?"

The sense of importance which had brought me through his door without waiting for his invitation to enter made me oblivious of a budding menace in his voice. "No," I said, "I'd wear a black and white one."

"Well," he said, "Go and get it."

I went into his closet, passing the shelves of shoes, the long row of cutaways and jackets hanging from their pole, to the stack of deep built-in drawers, the topmost of which contained neckties and dickies. The ties, neatly folded, made a colorful flooring that covered most of the drawer. I had to stand on tiptoe to see over the edge. I resisted a white tie with black stripes. One of black and white brocade-like material looked sumptuous and was also tempting, but I settled for one with small white stars, more nearly asterisks, and added to it another with a very thin white stripe. I was pleased when Father chose the one with stars.

"And do you know, Sally," he said, emptying his porridge bowl, "he was quite right. I'm astonished."

135

Mother smiled at me. Her quick ears had caught the rumble of the dumbwaiter in its swift ascent from the basement kitchen. That meant that Father's poached egg was on its way. To most people, serving a poached egg for a man's breakfast would seem a simple procedure. In the Edmonds household it was not. Father's specifications for his egg were relentlessly precise. The egg on its toast must have been cooked just long enough to be runny at the first touch of the fork; the yoke perfectly round and yellow; the white white, no trace of transparency was countenanced; the toast a moderate brown and perfectly flat, with the crust left on but, because of sensitive teeth, the crust must be softened by a trickle of hot water from the kettle; a *trickle,* mind you; too much water would reduce the toast to "quag." And the finished artifact had to be rushed the length of the kitchen to the dumbwaiter, where the cook slapped the lift rope and the waitress on the floor above pulled on the rope with such abandon as to set the pulleys squealing. Her quick steps pattered through the pantry, into the dining room, down the length of the table, and, pink-cheeked and breathless, she put the egg in front of Father.

After an interminable moment he picked up his fork and touched it to the yoke. It ran. A quiet sigh escaped my mother's lips, and the waitress, even pinker-cheeked than before, vanished without a sound. This was a good day. It had begun with approbation of my choice of a necktie; the egg test had been successfully passed. One felt that Father's day in court would be successful also.

How his day in court went I don't remember. In any event it is irrelevant. He had never lost a case, nor would he through the rest of his life. What mattered, at least for me,

136

was that from then on I reported to him in his room every morning at twenty minutes past seven to help choose what he would wear that day. The routine would continue unbroken until, five years later, I was sent off to boarding school.

Why twenty past seven, I do not know. Father liked life around him to function on an arbitrary schedule. From the moment I woke my eye was continually on my nickel alarm clock, which had something like a bicycle bell on top. What actually did wake me, however, at least on cold winter mornings, was not the indescribable, clamorous tocsin of the clock. It was the smell of coal gas. There was no movement, there was no sound, but all at once it was there, unfolding mysteriously, like a black flower opening in total darkness, stealthy, more than a little sinister. Under the covers a shiver would climb my back, while all the time I knew it was black Samuel (as my parents spoke of him), shaking down the furnace and opening the drafts three-and-a-half stories below.

We were only one of his customers on our block; how many other houses he took care of on how many other streets, we did not know, nor could anyone guess because he never said. He had his own key to the basement area door, which was underneath the flight of brownstone steps that led up to the front door. He would let himself in and pass along the narrow corridor alongside the bedroom that the cook and waitress shared, but they were never aware of him until they heard him shaking the furnace grates.

The furnace was in a small space of its own beneath the basement bedroom. A very narrow, short flight of steps led down to it and to another corridor that ran out beneath the basement entrance all the way to the street itself where, just inside the curb, there was a covered manhole down which the winter's coal was delivered from carts hauled by tired, drooping horses, This corridor was like a tunnel, with stone walls, and I have wondered since whether this tunnel might not have been the place used by the Weathermen who, in their bomb-making enterprise, brought down the whole house in what seems to have been a violent implosion. But that, like Prohibition, two World Wars, Nixon, and Ronald Reagan was a misfortune in the far and unthinkable future. In my boyhood quiet, self-effacing Samuel Ackerman took care of all this basement domain and kept us safe.

We children rarely saw him. Sometimes on Saturday mornings, he came up from below to polish the front door knob and knocker (once when I was maybe six, he vouchsafed, "To make them Sunday bright."). And invariably on Christmas morning, after all the presents under the Christmas tree had been distributed, first to the maids, then to us children, and finally to Mother and Father, Samuel would make his appearance, usually with one of his children, a very small black girl or boy, who could barely find a voice when bidden to wish Merry Christmas to Mr. and Mrs. Edmonds. The gifts to Samuel were always the same: an envelope from my father, which Samuel carefully bestowed in an inside pocket of the ancient Chesterfield he wore, and three yards of the best cheesecloth from my mother. This involved a small ritual, unchanged from year to year. Slowly, Samuel would take off the cream-white scarf around his neck, replace it with the three new yards of cheesecloth and, profusely thanking Mother, stuff the old into a side pocket of his overcoat.

In later years, when I had been a while in boarding school, I got to know him better. I found there was a lot more to Samuel than any of us had surmised. He was an avid reader, quoting often from the Bible, even more extensively from Shakespeare. And he could turn his hand to almost any task. All he needed, as he once told me, was a little time. He understood my parents and, I think, most other people, far better than they understood him. So, as the years went by, the whiff of coal gas, wherever I might be, inevitably conjured up the image of Samuel, a short, silent, ghostly figure in the basement darkness.

Once he had turned the corner from Eleventh Street onto Fifth Avenue Father moved into another world, or life. Still his world, his life, of course, or it would be when he reached his office. On his way downtown he invariably followed the same route, which over the years he had found to be the most direct. He was a vigorous walker, allowing nothing to distract him or delay his forward progress. This sometimes made for hair-raising incidents, according to my brother John, who, once in a while, had been invited to join him. Father would plunge across a traffic-jammed street, oblivious of rearing horses and their cursing drivers. Nothing stopped him, and on reaching his office his first act was to register the time of his arrival in a little pocket diary, together with the elapsed time between Eleventh Street and Maiden Lane.

On the door opening from the elevator corridor was gold lettering that spelled Edmonds & Peck, Attornies at

Law. It was not, however, a partnership, but a simple matter of convenience. The suite consisted of three offices and
a bathroom. Father, with his very active practice in patent
law, occupied by far the largest room. His secretary, Albert
Jenner, pursued his duties in a much smaller office next to
it. Mr. Peck used the third, almost identical to Jenner's. At
the end of the private hall was the bathroom, perhaps made
possible by the rent Mr. Peck payed Father. The nature and
extent of Mr. Peck's practice was a matter of conjecture; he
used the office sporadically, rather as a perch when he came
downtown than for work. But to a small boy he was an
imposing figure: a good four inches taller than my father,
with a beautifully tended dark beard that reached, as I was
at pains to notice, to the third button of his waistcoat, and
had a slight impediment in his speech that I found fascinating: it sounded like the underwater exhaust of a motor boat,
punctuating the running sound of his conversation. Yet he
remained on the periphery of Edmonds family life.

My father, though gregarious enough at college alumni
functions or in the life of the University Club, in both of
which he seems to have taken leading roles, was essentially
a loner. He never did have a working partner. He wrote all
his briefs on ruled yellow legal pads alone in his office or,
in the later summers of his life, in stylograph books in the
living room at Northlands. And that may have accounted
for their lucidity and the absence of legal jargon. Once (in
fact the only time) he took me with him to Washington,
where he was to file a brief before the Supreme Court. I had
had the notion that I would be able to watch him argue his
case before the full bench. But it was not that way at all.
Between breakfast and dinner I was left to my own devices;

apparently he wanted company only at those two meals. But on the last morning he took me with him to the Supreme Court building where we waited in a reception room for what seemed to me an interminable time, until finally a tall thin figure materialized in the doorway and Father rose to meet him. So I rose too, and we stepped out into the corridor, and the tall man said, "We have read your brief, Mr. Edmonds, and are impressed. We always are by your briefs. You make your argument in simple words that any man can understand. It is a pleasure just to read them."

A deep flush mounted to my father's face. He said, "Thank you, Mr. Justice," in not quite his usual voice, and I realized he was trembling.

Father's office had two windows with his desk between them and he sat so that the light came from his left. The desk light was an old brass, green-shaded student lamp that had been electrified by the time I got to see it. Both long walls were lined, floor to ceiling, with law books—set after set, they presented to my eyes a formidable solidity, almost a stolidity, like a huge conservative family making common cause against the adversities of life, a visual embodiment of one of my father's favorite phrases, "the power of the law." In their watchful but unseeing presence he composed his briefs, to be copied with dubious efficiency by Jenner on his up-to-the-minute Woodstock typewriter and so finally to be transmuted into the instruments that supplied the fees that fuelled our life at 18 West Eleventh Street and, infinitely more significant to me, kept the farm at Northlands in operation.

I was sixteen on that first visit, old enough to have some conception of the sheer, solitary effort that Father poured into making possible our family life. He might have become a man of real wealth if he had chosen to take in partners and build a legal firm. But he preferred to do it all alone, as if he wanted everything he did to be his personal gift to us. Or, perhaps, it should be put another way: he simply *had* to be the sole provider of everything we had in life in order to realize himself as a man—to know that his world and all the beings in it were his creation, and only his. And in these long-later years I wonder sometimes if that Jehovic posture, one might almost say conviction, of my father's did not contribute to my mother's continuous, un-diagnosed illnesses: the two and three stays a winter in hospitals, to which the doctors sent her so, as they put it, "she might rebuild her strength."

When my mother remonstrated about his going to the office six days a week, he would smile and say how else could he meet the bills. And when she asked with a look of both pain and shame, "Like my hospital bills?" he would answer, smiling (his smile was often genuinely sweet), "Among an awful lot of others, dear." As a small boy watching them, they seemed to exchange meanings impossible for me to understand.

At the office the first five days of the week were devoted exclusively to his practice. Saturdays the farm at Northlands held precedence and, whenever he had a really good man in charge, Father took an almost extravagant pleasure in following details. The superintendent, as Father called him, had to write weekly: his letter was a full report of each day's work and included a summary of the dairy herd's production, cow by cow. The birth of calves, of pigs, of lambs were all recorded: Father felt he had his finger on the pulse.

Yet he could be easily taken advantage of, as I discovered one spring when I was ten. An apparently endless series of colds, which none of our old family doctor's prescriptions seemed able to combat, persuaded Father that I should be sent to Northlands for a week. The therapeutic benefits of Adirondack air could not be questioned. Mother had doubts, but off I went, to be met at Boonville depot by the current superintendent, Meldrum Todd, a heavy-set, slow-moving individual, with a fulsome manner of speaking, though I hardly ever saw him smile. This almost superseriousness worried my father less than it did Mother probably because, as Father said, Meldrum certainly knew how to manage milking cows.

"We hope you'll be comfortable with us," Meldrum said, as we turned away from the deport. "We're giving you Evie's room and putting her in to sleep with her aunt. That's Mrs. Todd's sister. She came for Christmas." I thought he sounded a bit grim, but he added, "Evie is a restless sleeper." I wondered what Evie thought of the arrangement. I still don't know how it worked out, because I soon became absorbed in more serious matters. These started on our six-mile drive home.

Excusing himself each time, Meldrum stopped in at three different farms, asking me to kindly stay in the buggy to hold the horse while he conferred briefly with the farm's owner. I could not hear what they had to discuss, but each time, Meldrum Todd made an entry in a tiny notebook he had been carrying in his waistcoat pocket. This meant nothing to me at the time, but half way through me week at the farm Meldrum's little conferences began to fit into a picture that had begun forming in my mind.

The weather had turned bad. It rained nearly every day and, consequently, I spent most of my time inside the farm buildings. It was a time for calving. I also watched litters of pigs arrive: small black lozenges popping out at fairly regular intervals at what seemed to me no more than the blinking of a sow's eye. The first lamb arrived while I was still there. But by then I was using my ears as well as my eyes.

A small boy on a farm when events are accelerating can acquire near invisibility. So it was when leaning on the other side of a calving pen to watch the progress inside that I overheard more than one neighboring farmer who had come to visit with Meldrum tell him, "Yessir, eight of mixed feed, four of bran, three whole oats," or something similar, and saw Meldrum make an entry in his little book. And then another thing struck me as strange. During milking the three hired hands brought their pails to the end of the barn where the milk chart was mounted and a spring-scale hung from the ceiling and Meldrum waited to make the entry with the pencil from his waistcoat pocket. The hired hand would slip the bail over the scale's hook and call out his reading: "Daisy, twenty-three pounds and a half," or Beechnut, or Lady Collantha, as the case might be. But when, after Meldrum Todd had departed the barn to go to his supper and I had picked up the last lighted lantern and held it up to the chart, Daisy's contribution had miraculously increased to twenty-seven pounds, Lady Collantha's even more, while the small figures for some of the cows drying up had proportionately shrunk.

I didn't try to memorize the figures, for I realized it was the system rather than the actual amounts that mattered. And I was glad of this when Mrs. Todd insisted on helping me pack my bag at the end of the week, even turning out my pockets to whisk them, "so as not to carry barndust back to your Ma's lovely city home."

Father listened to my account without interrupting; then said, "You have done me a valuable service, Watty." Nothing else, but that was enough. Such words of approval did not often come my way. He knew at once what Meldrum Todd had been up to. That evening he sat down at his writing table in the library and wrote three letters to people he trusted in Boonville, and the next day made plans to go up to Boonville himself. But Meldrum Todd could smell a rodent as readily as anyone. On the Wednesday before his week end trip, Father received a letter of resignation for reasons, as Meldrum put it, of health. When in May our family arrived at Northlands, a new superintendent was in charge, and shortly afterwards my status in my father's eyes began to wane.

Not altogether, though. Having retired as superintendent at Northlands, Meldrum Todd built himself a brand new house in a conspicuous location on the way to town, wholly paid for, he was reported to have said, by profits from the best dairy farm in Oneida County. It riled my father every time we drove past it, though he did say now and then that if it hadn't been for Watty that house might have been half again as big.

145

In the next six years my relations with my father were marked by vicissitudes that might have been predictable to some but to me were mystifying, and in one instance terrifying. But in the winter of 1918–19 I realized that after three years I had had enough of the Episcopal boarding school that I had been attending in my older brother's shadow. I wrote my father that under no circumstances would I return to it, and why I wouldn't, and to my surprise he agreed. I think that for the first time he began to regard me seriously. At any rate, within a month he wrote that, after some investigation, he had entered me in a small (then) and much younger school and that I should take myself there the following autumn. He would, of course, continue to pay my expenses, but otherwise from now on I was on my own. Neither of us was to regret his choice. As the Choate School was in Connecticut and therefore much closer to New York, I was able to come home during the school year quite frequently. So it was that more than once I was invited to accompany him on his morning trips downtown.

Sixty-nine years old now, he much less frequently attempted the long walk, and never at his former headlong pace. On the first morning we set out together it was barely drizzling, but he judged it the precursor of real rain and said we would take the elevated. As we climbed the long stairs to the station he pointed out that it took more exertion than walking on the level. Entering the first car, he seated himself next to the door, but as soon as the train got under way he hopped up and let himself out onto the platform though a small sign beside the door said riding on the platform was prohibited. When I tried to join him, he forbade me fiercely. The platform was rudimentary, not more than two feet wide,

146

with a spindly railing, hardly waist high; but Father rode it, holding his walking stick against his chest, the cape of his coaching coat aflutter in the damp breeze, swaying from the hips as the platform swayed. Evidently it was a point of honor not to touch the railing.

Suddenly the brakeman appeared and accosted Father, pointing sternly to the door and the sign. I could not hear their voices above the clatter of the wheels. But from the increased color in his cheeks and the blue intensity in his eyes my father must have evoked the Declaration of Independence, the Revolution, the Bill of Rights, even perhaps the Gettysburg Address, all the absolutely no avail. His eyes positively glittered. Then, with a sudden hint of a smile he put his hand in his coat pocket. The brakeman took *his* hand out of *his* coat pocket. Their hands met in a green clasp. Father smiled, as did the brakeman entering the car. I wondered irresponsibly whether this was how our independence had been won, a thought that would have outraged my father.

For he revered our Founding Fathers; the Constitution was the Temple of his Gods; men, above all, who took up arms in defence of their country were his Heroes. But then there existed certain personal necessities and freedoms, like riding on prohibited platforms, the practice of which, in violation of his fiercely stated principles, raised no qualms in his ardent heart. Perhaps I was more nearly right than I then realized in thinking that it all depended on who did what. His patriotism was as unpredictable as it was idealistic. He wore it like the plumed helmet of Henry of Navarre. One never knew when or how it would manifest itself, as it was to later on that gray and drizzly day.

Being Saturday, traffic in Maiden Lane was sparse, the elevators and corridors in Father's office building virtually empty. When Father unlocked the door to Edmonds & Peck, we found we had the offices to ourselves. Father showed me over before taking me into his own office where, after hanging his hat and overcoat on the mahogany tree in a corner, he seated himself in his accustomed armchair behind his desk. I could not take my eyes off him. He looked right. He was wholly at ease. This, I realized all at once, was his true world. Where he belonged. Not 18 West Eleventh Street, with its domestic problems and worries created by growing children. Or at least such problems as our mother thought politic to inform him of.

A tin filing box occupied a corner of the desk, no doubt placed there earlier by Albert Jenner. "Northlands box," said Father when he saw me eyeing it. "I always deal with the farm problems on Saturdays. But I'd like to talk this time about something else." He opened a drawer, taking from it something I recognized at once as the Choate Literary Magazine: the first number of the year, the first publication in which any writing of mine had been printed. I had mailed it to him two or three weeks earlier. He had acknowledged receiving it but said he would discuss it with me the next time I came home. He had not mentioned it at dinner and I had been on tenterhooks all the rest of the evening. It was a story, called "The Wendigo," about an encounter on a mountain in Canada with the ghost of a murdered Indian, a chilling tale as my father had told it to me several years before and considerably more lurid in my version, and it had occurred to me that perhaps he resented my having made use of it without asking his permission.

But now, in his office, still holding the magazine, he smiled. "I've read it," he said. "I think you've told the story well. I'm pleased. I'm very pleased. It seems to me a splendid way for you to have made a start in your new school."

I felt myself go hot and full of prickles. I couldn't think of anything to say, which probably was just as well. For Father obviously did not expect me to say anything. He begun, almost dreamily, to reminisce about his own early days at Williams College. "I wasn't much interested in writing. Not as much as I was interested in public speaking. Debating. Anything to be talking to an audience. I made myself something of a reputation in the college. So when the Village Board came to ask the college if they could suggest someone to make the Decoration Day Oration, they were referred to me. So I delivered the oration and they liked it and the next year they asked me to do it again. They didn't bother to ask the college. They came direct to me. My senior year. 1874," he added with evident satisfaction. I nodded. The atmosphere in the office had grown intimate, one might say cozy. Being approved of by Father was a new experience. It took a bit of getting used to, but I enjoyed it.

He looked at me again and his eyes, usually piercingly blue, had softened—though whether towards me, or the college boy of nearly fifty years before, I had no way of knowing—and continued with his memories. "I accepted what you might call my first "case" that junior year. A young man in the village—he was known as "Little Milo" Nicolls—had been indicted for theft. His friends raised a purse for his defense and came to me. I agreed to appear for him. Williamstown's top lawyer, named Talmadge, appeared for the plaintiff. But I got him off." Father's voice had gained

149

a ringing note. "It was after my oration, and the jury were with from the start. Even so Judge Robinson complemented me on my presentation. We held a dinner of celebration, financed by my fee. That was the way we did things at Williams in those days. Little Milo had been invited so we could toast him. He behaved with unexpected modesty but, during the evening he managed to pick several pockets, including mine." Father's eyes dropped to the little magazine still in his hands. "After the eloquence of my defense, it did not seem appropriate to prosecute." He looked up at me, an inscrutable expression on his face. Or amusement? I could not think of him as sheepish, ever. His smile returned. "I suppose that might have been my first inclination towards the law as a career."

He returned the magazine with my story to the drawer.

"I think," he said, "I'll make this a short day. Let's go out and get an early lunch. Then you can go home and I'll come back here and deal with the farm papers. If it clears, maybe I'll walk home. Maybe look in at an auction room on the way."

Father loved auctions. The house harbored many of his acquisitions: an old French four-panelled screen, the tapestry fronts depicting a stag hunt, complete with horsemen, hounds, and fleeing stag, the panel backs of ancient golden-brown cut velvet which we children were not allowed to touch for fear our fingers would go through—(though it is still intact more than eighty years later); a small mahogany kneehole desk or bureau; an antique secretary, also French, with five secret drawers which I learned surreptitiously to operate about as soon as I learned to write. These, of course, were prize catches. And, indeed, he may have thought of them as he did of the splendid trout he used to take in annual expeditions up the Murray River in the Province of Quebec before his marriage. At the end of his office day he would break off the walk home to stop in at one lighted place or another to try his luck, as in former times he had cast over the deep, black pool in the next elbow of the river, the cold tension running from brain to fingertips, and back. One never knew. That was the actual lure.

So, today, he took me to an unpretentious small restaurant, "where the fish is especially good," where we had striped bass that for the moment overcame my youthful prejudice against fish as food, while he continued reminiscing—by now of his early New York City days, beginning with Columbia Law School, from which he graduated top man in his class. And afterwards he walked with me part way to the Sixth Avenue El. Near the top I turned to look back and saw his figure among other pedestrians swinging swiftly away, until he turned the corner at the end of the block.

———————

He came home late that afternoon, in a cab. His two-note whistling call for my mother from the front hall was immediately succeeded by a heavy metallic clanking.

"What can it be?" asked Mother. "What in the world has he brought home?"

We went to the head of the stairs. Father was already on his way up. He was carrying what appeared to be a large sword. Behind him came the cab driver, looking bewildered, carrying a second sword of a much different type in one hand and what was evidently a dagger in the other. With hardly a nod to Mother and me, Father proceeded along the landing to his own room where he flung the sword down on his bed. The cab driver followed suit, and the impressive clanking was repeated.

"Thank you, my man," Father said, adding an impressive dollar tip to the cab fare. The cabbie vanished in a second, his pleasure compounded by his evident relief. Father didn't even see him go. He was beaming on us and the three weapons lying in a jumble on his bed.

"A cavalry saber," He explained for our enlightenment. "Genuine Civil War issue. The other's also Civil war issue. Ordinary seaman's cutlass. The auctioneer said the dagger was of Italian origin."

I thought it the most interesting of the three. It was much bigger than I had thought of any dagger as being: two feet in length, perhaps even a bit more. The pommel at the end of the grip was of wire twisted to form a sphere, as were two similar but smaller like it at each end of the cross guard. The blade was broad, straight, tapering. There was no shine. To me it looked strictly business. I was impressed. But Mother was puzzled. Her delicate forehead wrinkled in dismay.

"But Gridgey," she asked. "What in the world are you going to *do* with them?"

"I know exactly what I'm going to do with them," replied my father. "I'm going to hang them on that blank wall over the head of my bed. The saber crossed with the cutlass, the dagger hanging straight down between them." We all stared at the blank wall, visualizing how it was going to look.

"I shall leave a note for Samuel," Father said, "to bring his tall stepladder up from the basement after breakfast tomorrow. We'll put them up in no time."

Sure enough, about ten on Sunday morning, Samuel Ackerman came up from the basement, stepladder caught on his shoulder. I heard his faint wheezing before I saw him materializing in the shadowy hall. He said good morning and continued up the stairs with Father's encouraging voice calling, "There you are. There you are, Sam. Come on up."

I was taking a midmorning train back to Wallingford to keep an afternoon appointment at school, but before I closed the front door I could hear Father's voice exhorting: "An inch higher, Samuel. Maybe half an inch to the left. . . ."

And Samuel saying, "Yessir, Mr. Edmonds."

Samuel's eye was infallible. The nail would be driven where it ought to be. And Father being Father would say, "He drove it exactly where I said."

When I came home at Christmas the swords and dagger were in place. I had to agree with Father that they looked well over the brass head of his double bed. I had outgrown my interest in doing valet duty, but whenever I did look in, he found an opportunity for calling my attention to his swords. Their presence obviously filled some deep psychological yearning. He may have seen himself as an obscure young naval rating repelling Barbary pirates with the cutlass or swinging high the saber as he charged close on Sheridan's heels. On the last morning of my holiday I asked him if he had ever noticed that the point of the dagger was black. "Almost like black paint," I said. Only, it would not seem to come off when I scratched it with my thumbnail. "It must have been there a very long time," I said.

"It probably has been," Father agreed.

"Almost since the dagger was made," I suggested.

Father again agreed.

I had been studying Medieval European History at school. My imagination started to take wing.

"I don't suppose it's as old as the Borgias," I said.

"I shouldn't think so," Father said..

"They used to put poison on their daggers," I said.

"Yes." Father's voice had faded slightly.

"I don't believe it's paint," I said.

"It's not likely," he agreed.

"More tar-like," I said, scraping at it once more.

Father had no comment.

"Curare is sort of tarlike," I continued. "Tar can dry very hard, I think. Whether it would poison a person when it's so hard I don't know."

"I shouldn't think so," Father said.

"But you never know, do you?"

Father did not respond.

To this day I have no idea what impelled me to raise the possibility of poison. Perhaps pure mischief. I'd thought of curare, naturally, because of reading "The Sign of Four" and rereading it more than once. I hadn't the faintest notion of whether the Borgias had ever heard of curare. But I returned to school with nothing on my conscience.

The next time I came home I saw that the dagger no longer hung between the saber and the cutlass. Thinking of our conversation, I was embarrassed to ask what had become of it. I did not see it again until some time after my father died. He had hidden it behind a stacked wall of hat boxes in my mother's clothes closet.

Children, too, can be cruel. Without even thinking.

John and me with Father, 1906. I always had trouble keeping my pants up.

"Father Is Dead"

{F} ather looked up from his Sunday chore of drawing checks to pay the monthly bills.

"Have you given any thought about where you want to go to college, Watty?"

I put the Sunday paper down beside me on the sofa and turned to face him. His desk was a replica of Washington's in Mount Vernon. Perhaps as he sat at it, he associated himself with Washington, as he did with so many others he considered heroes in history or mythology. But I did not see how, with Washington, this could be. Instead, I saw a much younger me drawing a check to myself and forging his signature. If, as was possible, the image occurred to him, he gave no indication of it.

"No," I said.

"I asked you to," he observed, "when you were home last time."

"Yes," I said. "I'm sorry."

Father seemed to accept this; there was no hint of censure in his voice as he continued, "You *should* be thinking about it. Your future in life will to a large extent depend on the kind of education you acquire and, as I see it, developments in science are going to dominate society for generations to come. I'd like to see you prepare yourself for a career as a chemical engineer. That's a field, too, that promises great rewards. In a worldly sense," he added.

I had no idea what a chemical engineer actually did; I still haven't. But the word "rewards" caught my attention.

"You mean money?" I asked.

Father bristled.

"There's nothing wrong with money. Not if it's honestly come by," he added in a somewhat milder tone, his eyes searching mine. "I've been doing a little asking around, and it seems that the best places we have for scientific study are the Massachusetts Institute of Technology, Rensselaer Polytechnic Institute, and the Stevens Institute of Technology. You've heard of them?"

I nodded. But Father continued to look at me questioningly. So I said, "MIT, RPI. I think RPI is good at hockey."

"I don't think hockey concerns us," Father said, impatiently. "MIT and RPI are older. By fifty years, I believe. But that does not mean that Stevens isn't good. Besides, it's much closer to New York. Just over the river in Hoboken. No trip at all if you take the ferry."

The Hoboken ferry had no special appeal for me but I knew better than to say so. "I don't think I'd be any good at science," I said instead.

"How do you know until you try?" he demanded. "I think you would, though. Look at the way you won a prize in that Wannamaker competition."

The Wannamaker competition was a scheme to promote the sale of Meccano, of which I had a modest set that I tinkered with by fits and starts.

Meccano was a construction toy: strips of metal in varying lengths with perforations at uniform intervals, angle irons, brackets, all to be joined with nuts and bolts. In addition there were pulley wheels and bars for axles, from all of which burgeoning engineers could build boats and buildings, derricks and cranes as their imagination prompted. In my day it was immensely popular among boys, myself included, and whenever I had saved up money, which was very rarely, I added to my original modest set.

After long head-scratching I produced a dump truck that had to be worked by a hand crank since I could not afford the key-winding spring motor that Meccano offered for boys who had financial means. But it worked and, though I was unable, with my limited supply of Meccano, to contrive a steering device for the front wheels, I delivered it to Wannamaker's four days before the deadline.

I was, I suppose, ten or eleven at the time. On the day the prizes were to be announced, I woke up feeling as if I was going to be sick. I was unsteady on my feet as I walked the two blocks east to Wannamaker's and became even more so when I arrived at the toy department on an upper floor. All the submitted models were on display and as I walked around the counters my heart sank lower and lower. The first and second prize winners were instantly visible, being mounted on elevated, slowly revolving platforms in the middle of the central counter, and also because they were much larger than any of the other models. I hardly looked at them. I had not expected to win either first or second prize. So I toured the other counters where every so often a model sported a white tag on which its ranking in the competition had been written. I did not look at them. I hunted my dump

truck. And all of a sudden there it was. And to my astonishment it wore a white tag.

I had won the twenty-eighth prize.

———————

I emerged from Wannamaker's in a state of euphoria;
but as I walked home I began to regard my triumph less
highly. A lot of the models I had passed over in my anxious
search for my truck seemed now, as I recalled them, considerably more ingenious, even one or two of those ranked
lower than twenty-eighth. My announcement to my mother
was almost casual. However, my voice sounded strained,
even to me. She looked up quickly from the sock she was
darning—one of my father's.

"Why, Watty," she said, "aren't you pleased?"

"No," I said, not knowing exactly why, and took my
way to my bedroom on the third floor.

Father, when he came home, would have none of this.
"What's the matter with you?" he demanded.

"It's only the twenty-eighth prize," I said. "In the bottom half."

"What's the matter with that? So your truck got only
twenty-eighth out of fifty. But you said models had come in
from all over the city. How many of them?"

"I don't know," I said.

"A hundred? Three hundred?"

"I don't know."

"Well, a lot. And yours was ahead of all that lot. And
you still don't think that's something to be proud of?"

"No," I said.

He stared at me, puzzled and clearly exasperated.

"I can't understand you, Watty."

"No," I said and, seeing that he had no more to say to me, went back upstairs to my room.

But his conviction that I had potential as a scientist remained unshaken.

"You would probably need a year at Stevens before you could decide which to concentrate in. Chemistry of physics. Chemistry would be my choice."

In his own mind he had already blazed a trail for me. It seemed better to say nothing. The idea of attending a scientific institution held no appeal for me. Having left a rigid Episcopalian boarding school where to "belong" meant to "conform," for another, less venerable but infinitely more liberal, my interests had turned to writing: not only for the literary magazine, but for the weekly newspaper. There the only assignment offered me was to report the Sunday sermons, almost always delivered by a visiting clergyman, since Choate, mercifully, was not a church school. The first sermon was so dramatic and I reported it in such detail, under the title "A Single Thistle Seed," that it was put on the front page. After that, if I found the sermon dull, I tried to give it life; whether in doing so the minister's original intent was tampered with or even lost did not concern me. So long as my story made page one, I was content. And my father was impressed. But that in no way altered his conviction that my future lay in the pursuit of science.

As it turned out, I did not need to worry. My brother suddenly stepped in.

John was older than I by only sixteen months but more mature and principled in every way. Where I had twice refused in a private session with the Rector in his study to be confirmed in the Episcopal faith, confirmation presented John with no problems at all. Though always much taller than I (who remained one of the shrimps of the school) he was not naturally athletic, but he worked hard at improving what ability he had. No one questioned his integrity. He was a member of the student council. He was industrious in study. He conformed because he believed in the school and was from his first year a "Saint Paul's Boy." In spite of myself I respected him. I had no idea of what he felt about me.

Both of us left St. Paul's in the spring of 1919: I to begin the first two years at Choate; he to enter Harvard. Though he never felt the devotion to Harvard that he did to St. Paul's (within hours of completing the last of his final examinations he was on the train for Concord, New Hampshire to apply for a teaching job at his old school) he had been deeply impressed and stimulated by the caliber of the professors he sat under, so, as soon as he heard of Father's intention of sending me to Stevens, he determined that I should follow him to Harvard.

"Don't under any circumstances let Father pressure you into going to Stevens," he wrote from Cambridge. "I'll talk to him at Christmas."

He did so, but without at first any effect on Father's views. From time to time I heard them arguing as I passed the library, their voices rising as each asserted his conviction, but neither able to convince the other. Through it all I hovered in an aura of neutrality, as if the point at issue did not in any way concern me. This, by the following fall, induced John to include me in his campaign, sending me clippings about Harvard from newspapers and magazines. He even went so far as to send me a ticket to the Harvard-Yale game.

The game did nothing to persuade me that Harvard ought to be the college of my choice, though it did open my eyes to the seriousness of John's concern, for the price of a ticket was a by no means negligible item in his tight personal budget. At the time, however, what really impressed me as I sat in my top row seat, was the immensity of the Yale Bowl. Though Harvard won—by three dropkicks, if I remember correctly—the game itself might as well have been between teams from Jupiter and Mars.

As I look back now, my impassivity that winter is incomprehensible. I took no part in their discussions. I did not want to. I cannot remember the slightest anxiety about which course my life would follow. I use "follow" advisedly, for in the years to come it was often my first impulse to take the trail already blazed. Again, looking back, I am inclined to think that after a time my future ceased to be the point at issue, or at least that they found their opposed philosophies much more attractive to pursue.

"Watty has a scattery mind," said Father. "The discipline of scientific study is what he needs."

"Perhaps," said John. "But your liberal education at Williams didn't hamper you when your turned to the study and practice of law. Williams *was* liberal, you know, in a way that neither even Harvard, or any other college in a city, can be. Good Lord! You not only had liberal courses of study, you had open country practically at your door!

You've told us how you kept a pointer in your rooms and went birding in the fall. You fished the trout steams outside the village in the spring. That's the kind of place Wat ought to go to. He's always happiest at Northlands."

"He never does any work at Northlands," Father said.

"Perhaps he doesn't. But he's happy there."

"There's more to life than being happy," said Father.

"Perhaps. I'm not so sure," John said.

So I came back into their seemingly endless debate, however dubious I may have seemed to either of them, and in the end, to my surprise, it was my brother who prevailed. It was settled that I should go to Harvard, though Father had not completely given in.

"He should study *some* science, at least," he said.

"He'll have to," said John. "Every freshman has to take one course in science."

"Then let it be chemistry," Father said.

"Of course, he'll have to pass his College Board exams," John said, a bit ominously.

I was not worried. My final year at Choate went well, my marks near the top of the class. I submitted stories to the literary magazines and had three accepted, as well as two excursions into verse, which was not as surprising as it might seem, since I had been elected "Managing Editor," though I cannot recall any "management" on my part. A boy named Eddie Parker was editor-in-chief. Hard working, enthusiastic, bubbling with ideas and energy, he left little editing for anyone else to do, so perhaps I can hold him responsible for the inclusion of my poetic efforts, about which the less said the better. As for my stories, it could be said that they were mysterious but not mysteries and reflected my fascination with Gaboriau and Poe. Good or bad, the exhilaration of seeing my work in print intensified with each acceptance and for the first time in my life I began to acquire a degree of self-confidence.

The year seemed to race by. The College Board examinations, when they came, presented almost no problems. My only mark under ninety was in solid geometry, which may have been a further indication that I was not cut out for a career in science. But with a grade of eighty-six, I did not need to worry about not being accepted by Harvard.

The intervening summer was not an easy one for, without consulting anyone in the family, John had taken a summer job in a cotton mill in New Bedford. To Father it was incomprehensible.

"I don't know how I'll be able to get along without John's help," he said to Mother. He looked bewildered and distressed. My brother's defection, as he began to call it, came on top of his discovery that his long-time secretary in the office at Maiden Lane had been systematically stealing money from the office funds for five years and his replacement had not yet gained Father's confidence. As a result he had been bringing his work to Northlands in the summer and my brother had been enlisted into making copies of his briefs. Father's backhand was difficult to read, at times so nearly impossible that a kind of divination was needed to decipher it, and John had proved adept. There was no typewriter at Northlands, so John made copies in old-fashioned stylograph books, writing on ruled, waxed paper over a carbon sheet which left an imprint on white removable underneath. Since the carbon paper was inked on both sides, it also left an imprint on the under side of the waxed sheet, easily readable and protected from smudging. The white sheets with John's highly legible, precise hand went down to New York to be copied on the office typewriter. But John, to whom Father paid his customary wage for jobs around the farm, was now in New Bedford.

"Working in a damn factory. Filthy air. God knows what kind of food he'll eat, sleeping in a tenement room, no doubt," said Father, "when he could be here, breathing God's own fresh air. I can't understand it."

His eyes seemed to pin Mother to her chair. She smiled gently. "Try not to be so troubled, Gridgey," she said. "I think he feels it's time for him to see a part of life that's different from our own." While the summer seemed to proceed much as usual, on the surface anyway, I became aware that something in Father had changed. He followed his daily routine of conferring with his superintendent, as he persisted in calling the farmer, even after the dairy herd had been reduced by two thirds. But his voice no longer reverberated among the buildings with its former resonance. Often he would cut short their consultation to walk up to the pond and cross the dam to the spillway to gaze on the fall of water for minutes on end, as if something in his life was lost or, at least, had been misplaced.

When Mother suggested that she should undertake the copying of his briefs, he would hear none of it. It was enough that she continue her management of the household, as she so beautifully did. The law, he said, was not for women, nor was any phase of the practice of it. In all this it never occurred to me to volunteer my own services. I had no confidence in my ability to concentrate hour after hour as John did. Nor, I told myself, with considerable truth, was my handwriting as legible as his. Nor did Father even hint that I try. But the actual fact was that I did not want to.

I think now, looking back after the passage of so many years, that John's decision to stay away that summer—his declaration of independence, one might call it—had shaken Father's belief in the rightness of his pattern for our family life, perhaps, therefore his belief in himself. Sometimes when our eyes met unexpectedly, his seemed to be troubled, almost haunted. But what was there to haunt him? Something in the past? That seemed unlikely, for his was a sternly upright character. The future? Himself? He was seventy-one years old, with just under three more years to live, though of course he, no more than any of us, knew that. But fear of dying never entered his thoughts. Of that I feel certain.

———————

I think it was my mother who missed John most. When, early in August, a letter came announcing his decision to continue at the mill until the Saturday before Labor Day and therefore not to come home—"It would be only for two or three days, hardly enough to justify the railroad fare to Boonville and back"—I could read her disappointment in her eyes. He was her favorite, as he always would be. She made little display of her feeling. But it was there; I could feel it, which made it all the more poignant. Not that she did not love our younger sister and me. There was no question of that. "He's doing what he thinks is best," she said to Father, whose answering comment I did not hear.

So, as two years before I taken myself to Choate, I packed my trunk and suitcase and set off.

As my train drew in to South Station late in the after-noon, I suddenly realized how little my brother had told me about Harvard. Beyond "take the subway to Harvard Square," I knew only that I had been assigned a room in a freshman dormitory called Standish Hall, number D-24. I was told at South Station where to find the Cambridge sub-way and at Harvard Square how to get to Standish Hall. It was one of three almost new buildings by the river. Some-one in the main entrance told me where to find D-24 and also the dining hall as well as the hour for supper. It could hardly, I realized as I let myself in my door, have been simpler. It is still harder today to realize the luxury in which I spent that first year in Cambridge. I had a study, bedroom, and bath, all to myself. My trunk was waiting for me. I unlocked it, opened the lid. That brought home closer.

I was still unpacking when there was a knock on my door and my brother walked in. "I intended to meet you at South Station," he said, "but I went to Ham's after signing off at the mill. He'd had a new speed boat delivered and wanted me to come for a trial run up the Canal. So I missed my train." He looked around with one of his cool grins. "They've given you quite a suite." I agreed.

He was living in Dunster Hall with three roommates. It was between the freshman dormitories and the Yard. He said he would take me there some day. Meanwhile he talked about the courses I ought to take and suggested I eliminate the required English A, a required, more or less elementary course in composition. "You ought to be able to pass their test." He grinned again. "And of course you'll have to take Chem. A, to satisfy Father. I'd recommend not taking philosophy. It's senseless stuff. A waste of time. You know where the dining hall is?"

"I'll find it."

"It would be hard to miss," he said, with another grin.

———————

Next day, after a brief session with my advisor, I signed up for my courses. Philosophy A was one of them. I did not regret it. Our professor was young, as it seemed to me professors at Harvard usually were not, and he opened doors in hitherto blank walls. His name was Raphael Demos and by my senior year he ranked in my mind with a handful of great teachers whose courses I had been lucky enough to take: Charles Homer Haskins, John Livingston Lowes, Charles Townsend Copeland. There were others, like Kirsopp Lake, whose lectures on the Old Testament I sat in on merely to enjoy a mind blown clear by fresh and sometimes boisterous winds. Or Roger Merriman—his course on European history was hugely attended more for the brio of his lecturing than the knowledge he dispensed. And the great gray eminence, George Lyman Kittredge, inventor of the Ph.D. In his Shakespeare course one studied two geniuses: the playwright and the academic work of art. Which ranked first was seldom in doubt.

Within a month I was enough at ease in my studies to turn once more to writing and towards the end of November I finished a story which, with considerable trepidation, I took to the rooms then used as offices by the *Harvard Advocate*.

One of the editors took it from me, asked my address and telephone number, which he scribbled across one corner of the first page in what seemed to me a cavalier fashion. But he was quite friendly, smiled, and assured me that I would hear from the magazine in a week or so. As I walked back down Dunster Street I realized suddenly that I had no copy, but I did not have enough nerve to return and ask for it back. It had a nonsensical plot about an old man who had trained his horse "backwards": to stop when told "Giddap!" and to light out for glory whenever he heard "Whoa!" Its virtue, if it had any, lay in its descriptions of the people and activities at a county fair, especially the harness races on its half-mile track. I called it, with singular lack of originality, "Jehu." Three days later my phone rang and I was told the story had been accepted and would appear in the Christmas number.

My parents seemed pleased and gratified, though I detected, or thought I did, some reserve in Father's praise, beyond his pointing out that in the Bible it was the driver, not the horse, whose name was Jehu. He did not say so, but he felt, I thought, that I should not use time and energy for writing that should be spent in study. That, however, did not deter me. As soon as I got back to Cambridge, I began working on a new one, by far the longest and most ambitious I had thus far attempted, about two brothers, grown men with grotesquely short legs, living on a canal boat with their grotesquely large mother, in a landscape of fens and fog and fantasy in no way related to reality, but extremely vivid in my mind. For two weeks, except for attending lectures, I did nothing but write. I called it "The Last of the Black Dwarfs" and when I handed it in at the *Advocate* offices I was sure I had produced a masterpiece, and when the magazine came out, both my name and the title of my story were on the cover. Within an hour I had mailed it to Father.

Nothing could have prepared me for his letter. "I am profoundly and bitterly shocked," it began. "It is inconceivable that a child of mine could imagine, let along *write*, anything so utterly vile. Almost every word is imbued with depravity and—it has to be said—lust. I am shaken to the core of my being. I shall not let your mother see it." There was more, but the ending shook me most. "Watty, I urge you to give up all thought of writing. Apply yourself with redoubled concentration to your studies. Our world needs people who will contribute to the values of life."

Apparently he wrote in much the same vein to my brother. I never saw that letter, but some fifty years later at Northlands I came across my brother's reply. "I am sorry you have been so upset by Watty's story. I know the language is pretty strong but I expect, if he is going to learn to write, he will have to work the eels and earthworms out of his system. Some of it is imitative and perhaps that's his method of learning his way around. The story was rather favorably reviewed by Professor Hillyer, incidentally, though I suppose that won't impress you. But I do disagree with your statement that if he is going to write, he should turn his efforts to the kind of thing that will ease the lives of overworked and tired businessmen. By which I suppose you mean stories like those of Jeffrey Farnol."

171

It was ironic, therefore, that thirty years later the citation for an honorary Litt.D. from Harvard should end with the words "a teller of stories that delight a wide audience of busy men." I was not aware of the irony at the time, of course, not yet having come across John's letter, but perhaps Father, wherever he may have been, nodded with some degree of satisfaction. Not, come to think of it, that I ever saw my father nod. Approval or disapproval, he always articulated his opinion, cogently and with force. And another aside: when I looked at the story again the other day, for the first time in seventy years, I found myself very much in sympathy with my father's position.

I had had my first real setback, and naturally there would be plenty more as the years flowed by. At the time my mind wobbled between bafflement, self-pity, and dismay. But the next day I started work on a story to enter in the *Advocate*'s short story contest for a prize of twenty-five dollars. The very number in which "The Last of the Black Dwarfs" had appeared reminded would-be contestants that the closing date was only ten days off. I delivered my manuscript with no time to spare, and it appeared in the Commencement Number, having won one of the two Honorable Mentions. My father acknowledged the copy I sent him, but without enthusiasm, for by then the grades for the final examinations in Chemistry A had come in. Mine, as nearly as I can remember, was thirty-seven. Whether this would mean an overall mark of D-minus or an outright E, I had no idea. For a day I agonized over ways of breaking the news to Father. I realized finally that there was no "good" way and wrote simply that I had been given a thirty-seven. It seemed pointless to say I was sorry.

It was *he* who wrote that he was sorry. His letter was singularly free of indignation or reproach. He seemed to have accepted my failure as a fact of life. "When you get to Northlands, we can discuss what your next move should be. I have an idea, but let's let it wait until then."

As it turned out, my grade was not so utterly disastrous as first appeared. I do not remember the number of students enrolled in Chem. A; it was, however, one the larger freshman courses, and now it appeared that only a handful of students had received marks above the thirties. So, by some process of rationalization or, one might say, one of those miracles by which the academic world insures its own immortality, the bottom grades were elevated and I, in all my scientific incapacity, received a final grade of C-minus.

But neither Father nor I was taken in. In science I had failed.

"I have given a lot of thought about what would be best for you in the immediate future," Father said. He paused and I waited, saying nothing. It had taken him several weeks since my return to broach the subject. I hadn't the faintest idea of what he might have in mind. Neither did my mother, whom I had discreetly questioned. It was a Sunday afternoon. He has suggested a walk around the pond, a favorite walk, following a path which, among others, my brother and I cleared each summer but now I did alone, wide enough to make a good shooting trail when he went birding in the fall and along which he had had a variety of benches built from which he could enjoy a view. On one of these, named

Pisgah, overlooking the head of the pond, we were now sitting. The vista, as Father liked to call it, provided an excuse not to look at each other. But when I did turn to look at him, his eyes met mine. They were concerned and unaggressive.

"I don't know whether you will agree with me," he said, "but I've decided that it would be a good idea if you spent next year away from college." He was silent a long time before he went on.

"It's my idea that you should spend the winter here at Northlands. No studying, but being outdoors every day, except when it drops too far below zero. You could help Henry with some of the work, like getting in the rest of the firewood. You'd stay in the farmhouse, boarding with the Schwartz's. I've talked to them and they will be glad to have you. I shall pay them for your board. All I'll ask from you is a weekly report on what you've done and what's going on on the farm. You'll be free to do what you want. The main idea is to improve your health, make your body stronger. *Mens sana in corpore sano,* " said Father, who liked to drive his point home.

I was bemused. "Well, what do you think?" he asked, impatience in his voice.

"I think I'd like to do it," I said. I felt that his emphasis on my becoming more athletic was for the purpose of diverting me from my writing. But already part of my mind was busy figuring out how I could use what had been the teamster's cottage, which in winter had no running water and, year round, only a semiattached privy (to my mother's continuing distress) for my study. "I think it's a good idea," I said, summoning enough grace to say thank you.

———————

It would be a winter of deep snow, and it began coming early. There were three inches of new snow the October morning that Hubie Morris came with a young beagle pup on a lead of old clothesline and said, "I've hunted with his Pa, who is a crackerjack on rabbits. I heard you was going to spend the winter here and thought you'd maybe like to have him. Paid twenty-five dollars for him up to Little Moose."

Twenty-five dollars took a chunk out of my small savings—I was neither industrious nor thrifty like my brother. But I was glad to pay Hubie for him and the dog became my companion and constant friend all that winter.

"You'll need snowshoes," Hubie added.

So under his guidance I wrote to Tubbs in New England for a pair of their Main Model snowshoes. "Tubbs are best," Hubie said with an air of brooking no dispute— not that I would have dreamed of doing so—and when they came he helped me rig them with a toestrap and rawhide thongs in the Indian fashion, lighter and less stiff and clumsy than a boughten harness. He also found a barrel out in what my father called his "Machinery Hall," where the corn harvester, the reaper and binder, and mowing machines were housed, a barrel that had once held kerosene. The smell remained, but not so strong as to dim the beagle's powers of scent. "And as sure as turkeys there won't no fleas stay

175

on him," Hubie said, nailing a board across the bottom to keep it from rolling when on its side.

In this way I was prepared from the start for the strenuous outdoor life Father wanted me to lead. But also I needed my study, not only to read and write in, but as a refuge from Henry Schwartz's very American and young and talkative wife, Jessie. I fitted out the small sitting room of the cottage, which was heated by a large chunk stove, with a small table, a kerosene lamp, the old Webley double-barreled shotgun with its Damascus steel barrels, a box of pencils, and half a dozen yellow legal pads on which to write my stories, that is such as came to mind.

Living in the farm house was pleasant. I ate well and Henry and Jessie were thoughtful people. She talked constantly about the baby she was going to have, though in the five years they were at Northlands the baby never materialized. Not that they did not try their best, as I could hear almost every night through the thin bedroom wall. In anticipation she knitted tiny socks and other suitable garments which, as she told me ruefully at times, she could always give to friends.

It was their first year at Northlands, as it would be the first winter for all three of us. Henry and I worked hard to get the firewood, twenty-five cords of it; fourteen-inch for the kitchen stoves, heavier eighteen-inch chunks for the parlor stoves, a smaller amount of two foot wood for the big house fireplaces and furnaces. Henry felt easy only when all of it had been stacked in the woodshed. He was right. I heard no wind during the night, only Henry and Jessie at their endeavors; but in the morning he reported fourteen inches— the first real heavy fall. We were not to see bare meadows again until the following May. In the woods it lasted longer, and in June there were still snowshoe tracks ten inches high where my most-used paths had packed it hard.

I went down to New York City to be with my family for Christmas but returned just before New Year's. In Boonville village five- and six-foot snowbanks separated street from sidewalk. Only a few years earlier, no effort was made to move the snow; it was packed down by a huge roller made of wood, five feet in diameter, pulled by a six-horse hitch, with three men driving, perched on top like three archangels in a row. In a hard winter there might be three feet of hard-packed snow come spring—something no automobile could hope to deal with. So, when for the first time the gasoline voice was heard in our land, the main highways had to be kept plowed.

However, once we left the Woodgate Road and turned into our own dirt river road, the going was in two tracks, formed by homemade plows that fitted over the right rear runner of a pung, or lumber sleigh. Each farmer was responsible for the road along his property.

It was a narrow, intimate kind of road, almost an elfin track, tracing its way along the river, through the silence of the woods.

I was glad to be back.

———————

When the wind was blowing and the thermometer registered zero or below, I wore a sheepskin teamster's coat as far as the edge of the woods where I hung it on a tree. Once out of the wind it was easy to keep warm. But the woods themselves had changed, something that puzzled me until I realized it was because I traveled on a different level, six or seven feet above the ground by the end of winter. On the open meadows surrounding the farm buildings the snow lay four or five feet deep, by Henry's measurement, packed solid and always with a crust, except after a fresh fall when it lay for a while soft as feathers. The cold thrust deeper as the winter lengthened, but in the woods one was aware of this only at times, as when a tree split from the frost, with a crack sharp as a rifle shot.

I wore layers of clothes, "light against the skin, heavy to the weather," as Hubie advised. Woolen breeches and heavy Canadian habitant stockings with the natural oils still in them, two thin sweaters over a flannel shirt and under a canvas hunting jacket, an old-time Balaclava helmet, and leather fleece-lined mittens with a trigger finger, from which my finger could slip back to join the others in the larger part. My beagle, whom I had named Diogenes for his wisdom in unraveling one from a myriad of rabbit tracks, was always with me, generally in pursuit of a rabbit or, I should say "hare," for we hardly ever sprang a cottontail. Our "rabbits" were Varying hares or, in the vernacular, "snowshoe rabbits," as much as four pounds, dressed, in weight, and in the winter snowy white and very hard to see until one learned to look for the black threadlike line that marked the outside edge of each ear. I now regret every one I shot that winter as mankind learns to regret too late the violence it does.

On those coldest days it was necessary to return to the farm buildings at the point in the edge of the woods where my sheepskin coat was hanging, stiffened from its long wait in the cold.

By the end of January the northwest winds had driven drifts against the north side of the house so high that with my snowshoes I could walk up onto the verandah roofs and look through the second-story windows at the upstairs front hall, where Mother's camphor chest, bought by a seagoing ancestor in China, held her best blankets safe from moths and buffalo bugs, and the corner cupboard in which I would find a treasury of paper bound books and magazines. But that came later, towards spring. Now I would walk back down off the drift and take my snowshoes off on the farm house porch and go into the hot kitchen, to sit, drink coffee, and talk with Jessie about what I'd seen, or might have seen.

———————

Towards February we were joined by Henry's grandmother, who had come from Germany to see her Americanized descendants. Northlands was her second stop and on her second day she volunteered the information that it was the first time she had not felt homesick. A compact little old lady, very neat in her dress, she arrived with her own yeast in a suitable yellow glass bottle and from then on we had homemade bread and rolls and the farm house atmosphere was transformed. She also had her own recipe for cooking hares: in a jug or, in our case, a crock, she marinated the meat overnight in herbs and vinegar (for want, as she explained, of wine) and they, too, were transformed. She admired Diogenes and in spite of Jessie's protests, admitted him to the farm house. When Jessie became too upset, pointing out that he was not yet housebroken (he never was reliably housebroken), the old lady would invite herself over to the cottage to sit with me and the beagle, and while she basked in the heat of our parlor stove, bring her crocheting out of her bag. By then I had begun to write a little, but her company was always worth an hour or two of writing time. She sat bolt upright in a rocking chair, her intense eyes fixed on mine while in her hands the crochet hook literally flew.

I had written two stories which had been accepted by the *Advocate:* one with an upstate setting, the other about a twelve-year-old boy left by his father in the hands of two villains on an imaginary island somewhere in the south seas. Now old Mrs. Schwartz, casting a sympathetic eye on Diogenes, said one afternoon, "You should write a story about your little dog."

That was something I'd never thought of. In a couple of days I had written a sketch, of four or five manuscript pages, and mailed it to a magazine called *Forest and Stream.* Within a week an envelope from the magazine arrived. They had accepted my sketch, now titled by the editor "Their First Rabbit," and enclosed a check for ten dollars. "We think there is a future for you in *Forest and Stream,*" the note that accompanied the check said. "We would like to see more of your work." The number in which the story appeared had a full color picture of a cottontail sitting upright in the snow, so that my sketch almost might be called the cover story.

By then a second sketch had gone off to the editor, Dr. Bruette, who had written that he would like me to address future correspondence to him personally. He liked the second piece and sent a check for fifteen dollars. This was a fifty percent raise. It seemed to me that I was on my way.

———

One morning, after a night of diamond-bright moonlight, with the thermometer registering thirty below zero, I came across something I had never seen before, in the alder swamp between us and the Hollins farm. It was a path beaten in the snow about six or eight feet wide that formed a circle perhaps thirty feet in diameter. Here and there along the perimeter I found individual prints of hares' feet—little snowshoe tracks along the edge as though their makers had been spun off by centrifugal force. I knew at once what it must be: the ballroom of a rabbit dance. Mr. Hollins had seen one once when he was in what he called his years of sprydom. Coming home after midnight from sparking a girl (he did not say whether the girl had become Mrs. Hollins) and cold enough to freeze a salamander's tits, he'd turned a corner in his snowshoe trail and there it was, right in front of him. Great white rabbits racing by him, one hard on another's tail—fifty? a hundred? of them, Lord knows how many, leaping like a mess of kangaroos. Never seen nothing like it before nor since. He'd dang near gone back to the girl's house then and there to ask her Pa to let them get married.

———

By now our winter had turned the hinge of February into March. Snowshoeing became difficult as warmer winds and the loftier sun turned the surface mushy and clogged the webbing of my snowshoes. I had to follow my most used tracks from one farm to another. In the woods there was an uneasy, sometimes disturbing sense of change. On warmer afternoons when I stopped to draw some easier breaths and let the beagle rest a minute on my snowshoes, I was aware of an indefinable ticking, like myriads of tiny clocks, unseen and unseeable, keeping time for the entirety of space. Now and then I thought it was the sap beginning to move beneath the bark. One afternoon, on the edge of the upland above the pond, the sound was louder, but not quite the same, and then I realized what I had heard was the trickle of a thread of water coming to life under the snow. When I emerged from the woods onto the home meadows, mist was drifting up the river.

It was the end of winter. Our coldest had been forty-two degrees below zero. Two other winters were to come when Northlands registered more than fifty degrees below, verified by an official weather station thermometer, and made the front page of New York and Boston papers. But for us the cold was over.

———

Father had been pleased to see my work in a professional magazine. Not as pleased as I had hoped, but I detected a warmer note in his acknowledgments of my weekly reports. A letter arriving at the beginning of April suggested that I come home for Easter. My mother would love to see me. "And," wrote Father, "why don't you see if you can catch something in the pond, if the ice goes out in time?"

Speaking of "going out," he and Mother would be having dinner at the Mastens, but my sister Molly would be at home to have supper with me.

On the morning of Good Friday I went up to the pond. I started fishing with a fly in the upper part where the pond made a bend like an S and in the first fifteen minutes struck and netted a trout that proved to weigh an even pound— larger than we usually caught. But one fish would not be enough, so after lunch I dug a bait can full of worms. I had been thinking about where to fish. The water was still roiled and muddy from the snow runoff and higher than normal, not ideal for fishing. But, walking up from the buildings, I remembered that when we drew the pond down there always emerged a large boulder, about two hundred fee above the dam, and when the water was completely down a strong-running spring could be seen bubbling out from under it. It occurred to me that maybe the spring would provide a bubble, so to speak, of clear water now as it provided an icy area in hot summer weather.

It took some time to find the boulder, but at last I did. I dropped the hitching weight that served as an anchor on the shore side of the boulder and dropped my worm on the deep-water side. Immediately, I had a strike. It was obviously a good fish and when I netted it I saw it was a good deal larger than the one caught that morning; in fact, it weighed a pound and three quarters. I waited ten minutes by my Ingersoll watch before I dropped another worm. Again the response was instant and I had another trout, smaller than my big one but larger than the morning fish. In the next hour I caught four more, all over a pound but, again, smaller than the first fish.

183

Still, seven trout that size was an unheard-of catch, from our pond.

Back at the farm house, I cleaned them and put them on a platter placed directly on the cake of ice in the Schwartz's refrigerator and then went over to the big house to find a box to pack them in. The kitchen and the parlor and the two flights of stairs leading to the attic still smelled of the winter's cold, and more strongly of the cow hair in the country plaster. The cold intensified the sense of emptiness. It was a relief to meet again the summer bat smell in the attic, but that too was transmuted, like echoes of forgotten laughter. I became aware of an aching inner loneliness so intense that I heard what I thought were ghosts. But in a moment I realized that it was the sound of shingles ticking as they expanded in the new warmth of the sun.

And suddenly, as was to happen two times later in my life when this same sense of loneliness and desolation assailed me, an object or a being materialized to bring my senses back into the living world. One time it was an eagle swooping not more than twenty feet above my head, the second time it was a young woman coming through my door. But this time what caught my eye was a seaman's chest, massively constructed of dark wood, with thick rope handles. It had been made three generations ago for a cousin, Admiral Philip Johnson, while he was stationed off the port of Valparaiso, and as befitted an admiral's belonging, it conveyed a sense of indestructibility and continuance that, just then, was infinitely reassuring. The attic, then the world took shape around it, and in a moment I found what I had come looking for, a tin box in which I could transport my catch of trout layered in ice.

I reached Eleventh Street in midafternoon. The waitress, Emma, who answered the doorbell, said that my mother was shopping and my father not yet returned from the office, but my sister was upstairs finishing some schoolwork, and, "What is it in your box, Mr. Walter? It's dropping water, I think."

She was quite right, and at her suggestion I took the box down to the kitchen and put it in the ice box, to the muttered expostulations of the cook as she shifted items to make room.

My sister had finished her work and suggested that I ride up town with her while she handed in her paper, so we rode up Fifth Avenue on the top deck of a bus and then back, and when we reached number 18 again, Molly came down to the kitchen with me to admire my trout. But they were gone.

"Sure, the Misther came back and I told him the fishes was in the ice box," Emma said, "and he came down to look at them and when he seen them didn't he run back upstairs and call a messenger. And when the young man got here, didn't your father pay him and give a dollar extra to be quick about it, too?"

I looked at Molly and she at me.

"Do you think," she said, "he could have sent them to the Mastens?" That's where he and Mother are going tonight."

185

I nodded. He had written me. And that's how it turned out. Mrs. Masten had taken special pains with her cook. The trout had caused a sensation, Father told us at breakfast. Mother smiled indulgently.

"Daddy was positively boastful about your catch and how Northlands could outdo Tahawus when it came to trout."

Tahawus was the fishing club in the Adirondacks under Mount Marcy where the Mastens spent their summers. The rivalry between Arthur Masten and Father went back over the years to their student days at Williams College, yet they had remained best friends. Now without question Father had scored a point. And Mother had seen my trout after all. I swallowed my disappointment.

Father's good humor remained for the rest of my visit. Then on my last evening he invited me to join him in the library after dinner. Mother left on an obvious pretext of helping Molly. We were alone among his Canadian trophies. Their presence reassured him, yet as he looked at me that evening, his eyes were troubled and uncertain.

"You'll be going back tomorrow," he began. "I think your winter on the farm has done you good. Don't you think so yourself?"

I nodded.

"You look much stronger," he said. "I think you're taller, too."

"Yes," I said.

"I'm pleased. I'm pleased also that you sold those two pieces to *Forest and Stream*."

I waited, with a vague feeling that he was just reaching the nub of what he wanted to say to me.

"I hope, however, you don't think that because you sold those two small pieces to a minor magazine you are qualified to follow a career in writing."

Again it seemed better not to say anything, though that was exactly what I had been thinking. And he probably divined this, for he continued, "When I graduated from Williams, I thought I was going to be a writer, to make my living by writing. But my father managed to dissuade me. He pointed out that many more men failed than succeeded at earning their living that way. Too often lack of success started them drinking and they became as useless to themselves as they were to others. My father knew two who, out of continual frustration, had killed themselves. What is more, he named them. I knew who they were, which shocked me more than their actual suicides. When he begged me to promise that before committing myself to writing I would try something else, preferably law, I agreed. 'Give it five years,' he said. 'You'll find writing enough in a legal career, and plenty to interest you, if you're any good.' So I did. I went through Columbia Law School. I've never regretted following my father's advice." He paused, then added, "The curious thing is that one of my college classmates started out as a writer. But he never had a success. And in a few years he committed suicide. I'd hate to think of you doing that."

I thought to myself that I would hate it, too. I was by no means convinced, but when he asked me earnestly to think about it, I said I would.

He stared into the fireplace as if watching subsiding flames, though the fire had not been lighted. "I envy you going back to Northlands now," he said, after a while. "I think you love it the way I do." (Not really the same way

187

you do, I thought, keeping a blank face.) "I've let myself love it too much."

His eyes were still lost in the fireplace as he searched his memories.

"The first time I saw it there was just the house, bare and rectangular, as Orange Barbour had built it, with the brook roaring past and across the brook a little ice house and the big dairy barn, not painted, not even clapboarded. But I loved it. The way it looked, the sound the brook made. I imagined the pond. I could see how it was going to be." He gave a small smile, a bit sky, almost sly. I did not imagine you children," he said. "But I tried to imagine your mother there."

He and mother went up to "camp" in the house in May after their marriage in 1901. As far as I know it was to be the only time they spent there by themselves. My brother, conceived six days after the wedding ceremony, was, of course, with them, but proved no handicap to their activities. They had a marvelously happy time as evidenced in a tiny diary she kept of those ten days. She was thirty, glowing triumphantly in the knowledge that she was pregnant. Father, at fifty, vibrantly in love, must have felt his own kind of pride. It was sad, as I read her buoyant words, to realize that such a time was never to be repeated, sad now as I looked at his white, white head and white mustache (on that spring visit in 1901 he wore a beard, nearly black, full, vigorous, but trimmed impeccably) that they had not *made* such a second time—spring, azaleas blooming in the woods along the pond, the two of them alone.

"I wish," my father said, "I had used Northlands in a different way. It's not a place for a big dairy operation.

There's not enough good soil. Crops wouldn't grow on the flats. Fertilizer just disappeared. Two or three weeks and it was gone. Down through the sand. The farm lost money: seven or eight thousand a year. Even more when Meldrum Todd was in charge. Even then I knew I ought to cut down the herd. But I couldn't bring myself to do it. I loved to hear the cowbells, heading up the clay hill road for night pasture. Coming back at first light in the morning." His eyes turned towards me, almost, I thought, pleadingly. "I know it now. I knew it then. But I was damned if I would do it." His face suddenly flushed, his blue eyes hardened. I understood. I too had loved the sense of living the big herd had brought to the farm. The sound of their bells, marking the passage of hours in each day, would be always there for one who knew when and how to listen.

I went back to Northlands next morning, taking the Empire State Express, as always, finding a seat on the river side.

My winter's absence from Harvard had removed my name from the list of students eligible for dormitory housing. I was told I should look for a room outside the college and given a list. But on my way across the Yard I encountered one of my brother's roommates, Owen Wister, son of the famous author, who had returned after his senior year to make a fourth and final effort to pass English A, the elementary course in composition his father had been instrumental in creating during one of his several terms as Overseer of Harvard College. When I told him I was looking for a place to live, he suggested that I return with him to his quarters on Church Street. The house in which he was living still had one unrented room. We lost no time. The landlady, a small, pink-cheeked, white-haired person, corroborated Owen: the room was still unrented; she would be glad to let me have it; I need not sign a lease unless her husband considered it necessary, and heaven knew when he would come around. I could move in as soon as I brought my bags.

As it turned out, Mr. Connelly did come around, stopped at my door, and bade me welcome. He was a Harvard personage: chief of the college police with offices in the basement of Grays Hall, a place I was fortunate enough never to have to visit. Like his wife, he saw no reason why we should have to trouble ourselves with tiresome things like signing leases.

So began my connection with John, the Yard Cop, as he was universally known. It was to last through my junior year when I occupied much larger quarters in his three-story house on Mount Auburn Street at the corner of Holyoke, where the windows of my top floor study overlooked the roof of the Spee Club, which, in party times, might present interesting scenes. There was nothing grand about the house on Church Street, however. It was like a small, village house, standing in what appeared to be an abandoned lot, its front section two stories high, with four small bedrooms in which we four tenants lived, with a one-story wing running out behind providing a large and sunny kitchen, as well as a bedroom I never saw, which Mrs. Connelly occupied, and, presumably, her husband on those rare occasions when he spent the night.

My room, on the ground floor, contained a bed, a bureau, a desk, a Windsor chair, and a washbasin with hot and cold running water—"a very great convenience," as Mrs. Connelly pointed out, for there was only one bath, on the second floor, with a toilet and a tub. The latter was of tin with a "mahogany" surround, long but rather narrow, in which our traveling salesman fellow tenant one Sunday afternoon got stuck, requiring Herculean efforts from Owen and myself, as well as piercing screams on his part, to extract him. Across Church Street loomed the parish house of the Unitarian Church, as well as the church itself, built entirely of wood, with a towering steeple that seemed to pierce the sky. On either hand and well beyond Mrs. Connelly's kitchen at the rear were the brick walls of three- and four-story buildings that fronted on Massachusetts Avenue, Brattle, and Church Streets. With one exception they were quiet neighbors.

The exception was the rear entrance to the new Splendid Cafeteria, from which every night around eleven o'clock were carried barrel after barrel of garbage to be placed in neat rows for clattering collection in the early morning hours. This practice was to affect my life significantly.

Sometime after midnight, cats from a wide area would begin zeroing in on the rear of the Splendid. I did not pay much attention, though I must have heard the wrangling voices through my sleep. But once wakened I could hear the annoyance, frustration, outright anger as they struggled with the lids of the galvanized iron barrels; then a frenzied outburst as a lid came loose and a barrel was thrown over, spilling its contents, and the quarrelsome pitch of their voices became suddenly the chilling clamor of a genuine battle. I could see nothing of it across the dark empty lot, but the voices supplied an image. It was no concern of mine. I got used to it and fell regularly off to sleep.

But it *was* my concern, as I was shortly to discover.

That night it was not the cats that woke me. It was the sound of rain. We had had showers fairly often, sometimes brisk, but never long. This, however, was a downpour, settling in like an equinoctial storm, and with the sound of pounding raindrops, overflowing gutters, there was something else: an odor, the smell of foodscraps out of a can, stale wet coffee grounds, in a word garbage, rank, close up (as reporters of the Olympic games of our day like to say) and personal. Moreover, a weight on my chest was holding down my bedcovers and myself. Cautiously I reached under my pillow for my pocket flashlight.

As I have said, my room was on the ground floor. The sill of my open window was hardly six feet above the stringy grass outside; but I have neglected to mention that we had no electricity. The light by which I studied was on the desk across my room. A broad, square base with a brass shaft in the shape of a Corinthian column, and a four-sided green and gray marbled shade. By all odds it was the best light I ever had to study by, but it did burn gas and to light it I had to use a kitchen match, which also was on the desk. I pressed the switch of my flashlight. The weight on my chest materialized.

It was a cat, old, ugly, and battle-scarred. I noticed two things about him at once: one ear had been shredded and the eye opposite, if indeed it was still in his head, had been closed. He was white, or what had been white when he was born, with patches of gray tiger marking placed irregularly about his body. Later, when he got up to leave, I saw that his back had been permanently injured, perhaps in a dispute with some sort of delivery van, so that his hind feet did not track with the front. He was so ugly that I named him Quasimodo.

As I played the flashlight around my room, I saw other cats ensconced in varying attitudes on my chair, desk, two more besides Quasimodo on my bed, one curled with apparent comfort in the basin; ten, perhaps a dozen of them, most with scars from earlier wars; but none exuding the sheer ferocity of the misformed gray and white monster on my chest. Towards morning, as the rain eased, and the first hint of dawn picked out the towering wooden steeple, he came to his feet. So, in silence, did the others. He dropped to the floor, lifted himself to the windowsill, and was gone. The others followed, disappearing over the sill, soundless as a flow of water.

In the morning I asked Mrs. Connelly if I might have a screen for my window. She looked dubious but promised to ask Mr. Connelly. She was right to look dubious. Mr. Connelly saw no reason to provide a screen. It was too cold now for mosquitoes. Cats were no concern of his. If they were troublesome, why not simply close my windows? Which, on the next rainy night, I did. But Quasimodo and his co-horts raised such a clamor of lament and outrage that I gave up. As soon as I lifted the sash they came pouring in to assume their accustomed places. And so my winter, on Church Street, was to go.

In the Yard it went well. I was excited by my courses, particularly those given by Professors Lowes and Haskins: the first on the Romantic Age in poetry, the second a half-course on medieval living. I found each totally absorbing. They so filled my mind that I found myself thinking of them at odd times during the day, even while listening to other lectures. Undoubtedly they were factors in my steadily intensifying urge to write, which now, as I think back to that winter, had become almost all-consuming.

Altogether, I produced six stories for the *Advocate* between September and May. Two won the P. W. Thayer Prize, which had recently been given for the best annual contribution to the *Advocate*. As the Thayer Prize was offered for two years only, nobody else ever won it. That troubled me; it still does. But my doubts were less important to me than the hundred dollars that accompanied each award. It bolstered my still-shaky confidence that somehow there was a living to be made out of writing, as out of any other exercising of the mind.

One of these stories was set in Paris in the time of the poet Villon. Surely it was inspired by Stevenson's story "A Lodging for the Night," yet it was pretty much my own. Called "St. Bon and the Organist of Midnight Mass," it told how through a set of circumstances an old musician, an organist, who had fallen on evil days, a drunkard, through the intervention and inspiration of the saint, played in his church on Christmas Eve. It was much my most ambitious effort but, as I recall, its significance in my work as a writer lay, for the first time, in my doing some research. I was hardly into the writing before I was seized by the absolute necessity of knowing where I was.

Somewhere, in what book I simply can't remember, I came across a map of fifteenth-century Paris and copied it. I found books that gave me some idea of how various classes lived, ate, drank, dressed. My approach was anything but systematic, I picked up a bit here, a bit there, like a crow, and flew back with them to my roost in Church Street. Early in November, as I was finishing the story, it rained. The cats appeared in the heat of my writing. They assumed their accustomed stations. With the two regular desk-sitters in place, there was not enough room to spread my maps and notes. I had been lucky to pick them up before the two dripping and garbage-scented bodies could land on them. I was nonplussed. Any forcible effort to dislodge them would meet resistance of a sort I had no notion of inviting. As I looked at the faces around my room, most of them scarred from earlier conflicts, or, if not scarred, experienced beyond imagining, I knew that the least attempt to assert my rights would spell disaster. They were like the Musketeers: an attack on one would be an attack on all. But on the other hand I was hot to finish my story.

How long our standoff might have continued is anybody's guess. *I* did nothing to resolve it. The first move came from my bed. With a low, almost gentle, bubbling utterance, Quasimodo came to his feet. All of us, cats and student, turned towards him. Without looking at any of us, he dropped lightly to the floor, crossed the carpet, and jumped as lightly onto the desk. He looked directly at the two sitters and reiterated that soft and gently wistful note. The two cats got the message. With no remonstrance they left the desk and joined the two others at the foot of my bed. Quasimodo glanced at me, did one modest revolution, and curled up on the very corner. In a moment I had respread my papers and resumed writing, and finished the story two hours later. It did not occur to me that Quasimodo's contribution deserved an acknowledgment. But then few people would have believed me. Fewer still are as perceptive as cats.

———————

My father considered the story an advance, though he deplored my continuing "fascination with the lower order of mankind." And why did I have to end on such a note of cynicism? A Christmas story should offer a message of hope, of well-being, even joy. There was nothing of that, only a morbid return into drunkenness. It was regrettable, especially since so much of the story was vividly told. Even a suggestion of something better for old Nicholas would have added lustre to my story.

On the whole I was pleased. I thought his letter sounded as if he wanted to like the story but was prevented from doing so more from habit than conviction. Of course, at that time, I knew no more than he that it would win a prize. And already I was at work on the story that would bring me my second Thayer Prize.

It was published in the March number, a simple tale of a country boy, made restless by the coming of spring, deciding to leave the country on a canal boat bound for Rome where our Black River Canal joined the Erie Canal which was then the major continental artery of east-west domestic trade and, indeed, of international trade as well. For rural boys it was the road to adventure, wealth and what seemed the true reality of life.

I was chiefly interested in portraying the end of a northern winter of deep snow, the step by step unlocking of the earth that ended with the breakup of the river ice, when massive sheets, fifteen or twenty feet across, would be up-ended on the rapids and fall with booming crashes that could be heard a mile away. Father, who for all his Utica boyhood had never experienced a winter's ending in the open country, was stirred, even impressed. It was the first piece I had done for the *Advocate* that he really liked. As I have said, it also won the Thayer Prize and in addition would win a second prize (two second prizes were awarded) in Harper's Intercollegiate Short Story Contest the following year, though, to keep the record straight, it was the only winner Harper's Magazine elected not to publish.

But these things came too late.

Spring in Cambridge was nothing like that Northlands spring. For one thing it did not follow months of deep and lasting snow. It came quietly. Snowdrops, crocus, little drifts of scylla near house foundations on Brattle Street, then flowering trees: magnolias, dogwood, Judas trees, with for-sythia burning yellow underneath. Spectacular, but they lacked the mystery of the white, fragile clouds of shadblow appearing overnight here and there along the edges of the woods; or the wild azaleas, the pinxster, in honor of which in Colonial times the Dutch burghers of Albany, New York, declared an annual holiday on which, with wives and children, they took picnic lunches into the woods to enjoy the sweet, pervasive fragrance, returning at evening laden with bouquets to perfume, for an additional night, their step-gabled houses.

What birdsong one could hear above the traffic was different, too. There was nothing like the wave of song that filled our northern woods while the warbler migration was in progress.

When I had Sunday evenings free, I extended my walks into Boston to have dinner at restaurants like the Amalfi, on Westland Avenue, or the Olympia on Stuart Street, not because of a special liking for Italian or Greek cooking but because for a little over a dollar I could get a whopping big meal. Later a friend introduced me to an Italian restaurant called La Grotte Azura, whose Veal Coltiletti à la Milanese I still remember as well as their way with sole. It was there, also, that my friend and I talked for the first time about the possibility of writing a novel about life on the Erie Canal in its heyday.

He came back to my ground floor room on Church Street and we talked about the novel some more. His name was Merle Colby; he was enthusiastic. "What," he asked, "did they call a trip from one place to another?"

"I don't know," I said. "A haul, I guess."

"The Syracuse haul," he said, musingly.

"Rome would be a more important town for boats from our Black River country," I said.

"The Rome Haul," Merle said. "No. No 'the'. Rome Haul. That's it."

I had the title and two more years of talk about the book during college, but it was four years before I wrote it.

Spring in Cambridge may not have been much like spring in upstate New York, but there were times when life began to seem within my reach and things were beginning to come my way. Feelings like those are the kind we have to pay for.

April was nearly at its end. I had finished another story and had only to make a clean copy before taking it to the *Advocate* and had begun to think about final exams, though they were still nearly a month away.

I got ready for bed, then went to my window and opened it wide, for nights were getting warmer. A really light rain had begun to fall, more mist, actually, than rain. I wondered if it would get wet enough to bring the cats. I could hear them starting to work on the garbage cans behind the Splendid. Their voices sounded almost amicable as I drifted off to sleep.

Noise at my window woke me. At first I thought it was the cats. But it persisted, a scraping, scrabbling sound, and much too loud to be cats. I found my flashlight and pointed it towards the window. The head and shoulders of a man appeared and when he turned his face to the light, I saw it was my brother, John. He had graduated in March of the winter before, finishing in three and a half years and had gone straight back to Concord, New Hampshire, and St. Paul's to apply for a job on the faculty. And what is more, though there was no room for him in the French department, he was offered a job teaching German and took it.

Such enterprise, such successful enterprise, had seemed to me admirable, though St. Paul's was the last place in which I would have wanted to spend my life.

We spoke together.

"What is it?" I asked.

"Wake up," he said, superfluously, it seemed to me, but added, "Mother telegraphed me to come home and to bring you. Father is ill, dangerously ill. Put some things in a bag. I have a taxi waiting on the street."

While I dressed and packed a suitcase, he told me Father had pneumonia; had had it for several days but Mother, typically, had not wanted us to worry. He picked up my suitcase, I closed the window, and we went out to the waiting taxicab. John did not have to tell the driver to take us to the South Station.

There we bought tickets and John explained why we had to get to New York as quickly as possible. The agent called the stationmaster's office. There was no problem. We were given a paper to show and told where to find the mail train, due to leave in fifteen minutes. It had one rather threadbare day coach at the end, but there was room to spare with only members of the train crew and ourselves.

We didn't have much to say to each other. The train crew, such as appeared, gave us sympathetic glances but few words. What I remember best are the locomotive whistle for the crossings, long drawn, peremptory, infinitely sad.

———

No taxicabs were waiting on the rank, but one came cruising in before we made up our minds to try our luck on

Forty-second Street. At that early hour we saw hardly a car or, for that matter, a bus on Fifth Avenue. Our driver was talkative. He asked if we were home from school. Looked like school, well maybe college, boys to him. My brother stiffened, but remained silent. I said I was in college but that my brother was a teacher. Our driver let it go at that. All three of us remained silent until we turned the corner by the brownstone Presbyterian church into Eleventh Street and pulled up at number 18.

"Father is dead," John said.

Something churned over in my inside.

"You don't know that," I said.

"Look at the front door," said John.

The black front door looked as it always did, to me.

"The bow," John said impatiently.

"Yeah, that crêpe bow on the handle," our driver said. "Always means a dead one."

John paid our fare without speaking and went up the brownstone steps. I followed, I did not know why I hadn't seen the black crêpe bow on the door handle. It seemed beautifully, lovingly tied. John rang the bell. In a moment the waitress opened the door. We went in.

The house had always been a quiet one—except in early times when on rainy days we children roller-skated in the third floor hall. But now there was a hush. I felt it even when I went into the sunny library and sat down at his writing table in my father's chair. John had gone upstairs immediately and now, with a sense of shock, I realized that I should have gone up with him. I did not know why I had not. I continued to sit, not stirring, without conscious thought, until I heard Mother's voice on the upstairs landing.

"Watty," she called.

"I'm coming," I said.

John was beside her, looking at me as I came up. His face was totally without expression.

Mother put out her arms.

"You were wonderful to get here so early."

"John arranged it," I said.

"You and John, then," she said. "My boys."

As she sometimes used to say. Only then it included Father.

"Come into my room," she said, and in her sunny window she told us how he had died, peacefully, puffing a cigarette she had rolled for him after the doctor said he was over the pneumonia.

"He's in his bed," she said. "If you would like to see him." She glanced at the small carriage clock that used to be grandfather's on her mantelpiece. "They will be coming for him in about an hour."

I got to my feet and glanced questioningly at my brother. He shook his head.

"No," he said. "I'd rather remember him the way he was."

His voice was clear, precise, colorless, as if he was dismissing a class.

Mother looked at me, not him. I had no idea what she was thinking, but her eyes followed me as I left her room.

I went along the landing to Father's room at the front of the house and, with my hand on the door handle, hesitated. I had never seen a dead person. It seemed strange that the first should be my father. I wished for a moment that I had replied as John had. It would be possible, even now, to wait a minute or two and then go back and say that I had seen Father. But I knew that would not do. Not because I would be lying. I was under a compulsion of my own.

I had to say good-bye.

I turned the knob and went in. The windows had been closed and the shades pulled down, muting such sounds as came from our quiet street, intensifying the silence I had become aware of downstairs.

He lay on his brass bed, the covers drawn up to his chest, his hands and arms outside them. His eyes were closed. His face was marble white, so white that the usually white, white mustache looked ivory and gray. The stillness of his body was absolute.

As I looked down at him he seemed much smaller; no more the forceful, overbearing character that, through all our earlier years, had ruled our family life. The features had not altered. They were still handsome, strongly cut. But beneath the mask I now saw, or thought I saw, hesitance, self-doubt, almost a fragility of purpose, and wondered if it had not been there always. He had wanted to excel. He had. He had never lost a case in his long legal career. But standing by his bed, looking down at him, the image came to me of a man running scared. Not of adversaries, in the law or anywhere else, but of himself. Of failing to measure up to his conception of what made a man.

I glanced at the wall above his bed. The swords were still in place; the dagger was still absent. I nearly smiled but at the same time felt ashamed of what had then seemed merely funny. There was no indication in the dead face that he had ever thought of it again. I realized how vulnerable he had been, how vulnerable at other times when he successfully concealed his weakness.

An overwhelming surge of love swept through me. I bent over and kissed the white forehead.

Silently, I said good-bye.